Did You Eat Yet?

Did You Eat Yet?

CRAVEABLE RECIPES
FROM AN ALL-AMERICAN ASIAN CHEF

RONNIE WOO

HARVEST

An Imprint of WILLIAM MORROW

HarperCollins books may be purchased for educational, business,
or sales promotional use. For information, please email the Special
Markets Department at SPsales@harpercollins.com.

FIRST EDITION

Designed by Laura Palese

Library of Congress Cataloging-in-Publication Data has been
applied for.

ISBN 978-0-358-58169-7

23 24 25 26 27   IMS   10 9 8 7 6 5 4 3 2 1

Introduction

I'm a model turned therapist turned globetrotting chef who also happens to be Asian, American, and gay—each of which I'm 100% proud to be,

making me 700% amazing (I was never a math guy, so just go with me on this one). My parents told me to become a doctor or lawyer (shocker!), but let's just be honest here: they were really setting me up to become a chef thanks to the constant chatter about how much they loved eating. I grew up in a family where every dinner was spent talking about what we were going to eat for the *next* dinner. My mom would wake up early and cook different dishes for lunch, like Chinese sausage fried rice or an egg omelet sandwich, just so she could send all of us out the door with a homemade meal packed in one of her various Tupperware containers. And when I got home, there was always a snack waiting for me (with my two favorite snacks being either my mom's homemade wontons or Totino's Pizza Rolls). All our family vacations were planned around whichever location on earth had the best food. If a destination wasn't known for the food, it was out of the question. I know it sounds like my family and I were gluttonous giants eating everything in our path, leaving only a trail of chicken bones and orange peels, but the truth is food is just my family's love language. Whenever I call or visit Mama Woo, the very first thing that comes out of her mouth is, "Did you eat yet?" Those four simple words have always made me feel loved, welcomed, and cared for, and since it's the same exact thing I would ask if you were at my house, making it the book title was a no-brainer.

I've worn many different hats in my life and each of those chapters has played an integral part in the process of how I got here. I mean, where do I even begin? Thanks to an awkward growth spurt in high school, I started modeling when I was a teenager, eventually moved to LA, and got to do some pretty amazeball modeling gigs. Along the way, I also became a certified personal trainer and even though I absolutely hated working out, it was kind of fun telling people what to do. Yes, I know exercise is good for my physical health, well-being, and blah-blah-blah—but I'm not going to lie to you, the only reason I work out now is so I can eat more.

After living out my dreams as a glamour puss (a.k.a. male model), I decided to go back to school. I got a BA in psychology and, like any other good, overachieving Asian kid, I went on to get two master's degrees, an MBA and MFT, while simultaneously working at a mental health clinic. This also happened to be around the same time that I met my husband, Doug. I was high on dopamine and adrenaline from being in loooooove and I felt like I could do anything. So, I decided to further explore my love of food and cooking and just went for it.

Whenever I call or visit Mama Woo, the very first thing that comes out of her mouth is, "Did you eat yet?"

I had never felt more empowered or confident about anything in my entire life. I always knew I loved eating, but now cooking had become my true happy place. I dedicated every day to being in the kitchen, teaching myself to cook everything and anything under the sun, and doing my best to refine my culinary skills. Shortly thereafter, I launched my private chef company, The Delicious Cook, which specialized in personalized intimate dining experiences, typically consisting of multicourse dinners in clients' homes. I found myself working with some of the biggest names in Hollywood and quickly established The Delicious Cook as one of the most sought-after private chef companies in the entire universe (at least from what I've heard). Having cooked for every type of personality imaginable and in home kitchens of every size, I've racked up years' worth of insight on how to make mouthwatering dishes in the comfort of your own kitchen that still bring that "je ne sais quoi" (which is French for "awesome-ass deliciousness").

I've had the wonderful privilege of continuing to travel the world for the sole purpose of finding the best food. With each new experience, I've come to learn that cultures and cuisines are constantly influencing one another, evolving, and changing over time. What may be authentic to you might not be authentic to someone else, and that's what makes the world of food super-duper fun. Some of the recipes in this book might be more traditional than others, like the minced beef and rice bowls on page 81 or the chicken congee on page 198, while some are interesting combinations of different flavors and cuisines—such as my Spicy Almond Pesto Udon (page 106) or Crab Cake Pot Stickers (page 141).

I've never fit into a single box, and neither do my recipes. Much like myself, this book is akin to a gloriously stacked dim sum cart at Sunday brunch—there is something for everyone—and I know you're going to find a buttload of recipes you'll want to make and devour (if not all of them). What every one of these recipes has in common is that they're damn delicious, bursting with flavor, and made with accessible ingredients. I'll never tell you to buy a superfluous one-time-use ingredient or add unnecessary steps. Don't get me wrong; it's not about cutting corners but rather consistently making an irresistible fail-proof dish. I promise that each one of these recipes will excite you, titillate your taste buds, and hit the spot!

In the mood for an Asian-inspired dish? I've got you, boo. Feeling kind of healthy? Fear no more, you've got options! Want a downright delicious noodle dish? There's an entire chapter dedicated to them. Want to try your hand at making pot stickers? I'll walk you through it fold by fold. Looking for a decadent dessert? Of course! This book has it all.

There are many reasons why you might have this book in front of you. Maybe you were hungry, saw the cover, and thought to yourself, "That food looks scrumdiddlyumptious!" or "That Asian dude looks like a nice person, please take my money." Maybe you're one of my longtime fans. Or maybe someone who loves you very much gifted you this marvelous book. Whatever the reason, I just want to say thank you. I swear on the Lord's dumplings that you are in for a real treat. I love feeding people and it's how I express my love, but since I can't personally cook for every single human on this planet (as incredible as that would be), writing a cookbook is the next best thing. Whether you're cooking out of these pages for your family and friends or it's a table for one, just be warned that you're going to have a hell of a lot of fun making these recipes and even more fun eating them. You might even get a chuckle or two out of the stories as well—which is a win-win because laughing is like jogging on the inside. If for some reason you end up hating this book, don't tell anyone and just pretend that it is the most brilliant cookbook you've ever owned. Thanks!

And since you're here, let me ask you something—did you eat yet?

Be warned that you're going to have a hell of a lot of fun making these recipes.

First Things First

Whether you are a humble culinary peasant who has found a way to burn instant ramen or a professional chef who has cooked with the tears of virgin unicorns, I am confident you'll learn something from this book. And even though I firmly believe that there shouldn't be any rules in the kitchen, here are a few suggestions, explanations, and tips that will make your time spent in the best room of the house even better. Lastly, if I ever do a sh*t job of explaining something, you need a video tutorial, or just want more information, just click them keys and find it on the internet.

Mise en Place

Mise en place is a French culinary term that means "to put in place," and it's going to prevent you from looking like a fumbling boob multitasking between prep and cooking. To simplify it, let me break this down into three parts:

1. ***READ THROUGH THE RECIPE*** Before you do anything else, read through the entire recipe, both the ingredient list and the instructions. This way, you will know what ingredients and tools you need, in addition to when and how you will need them, so nothing will catch you off guard.

2. ***GATHER WHAT YOU NEED*** Gather the necessary equipment and tools, prepare your ingredients (wash, cut, chop, dice, mince, measure, etc.), and organize your workspace.

3. ***START COOKING*** Now that everything is ready to go, you should cook, cook, cook! One last thing I suggest is to clean as you go (or have your lover, friend, or children do it). Cleaning as you cook will help keep your workspace organized, save you time, and, if you're like me, keep your anxiety level at a minimum.

Pantry Staples

Searching for hard-to-find ingredients is one of my favorite pastimes, right behind poking my eyeballs out and eating a piece of stale bread that I later regret because it wasn't worth the carbs. What I'm really trying to say is that I'm not a fan of hunting down ingredients, so almost everything in this book can easily be found at your local grocery store. As for the handful of ingredients that might be more specialized, head to your local Asian supermarket or hop online and you'll have them in no time. As you begin to spend more time in the kitchen, you'll build your own set of pantry staples. However, if you need help getting started, here are some of the ingredients that can always be found in my kitchen.

Rice: The Best Carb in All the Land

You'll always find dry rice in my pantry and frozen cooked rice in my freezer because every human being I know loves rice and even a little goes a long way. Rice is every dish's BFF, it's easy to make, and it's a crowd-pleaser. My general rule of thumb is that if a recipe calls for a specific type of rice, you should try to stick to it. Otherwise, it really boils down to personal preference. Here's a little breakdown of the main types of rice and how to cook them:

SHORT GRAIN VS. LONG GRAIN

- *Short-grain rice* is starchy, cooks up moist and tender, and the cooked grains tend to stick together. Sometimes short-grain and medium-grain rice get put together in the same group, and in general I've had pretty good luck using these two interchangeably.

- *Long-grain rice* is much less starchy, cooks up dry and firmer, and the cooked grains tend to stay separated.

BROWN RICE VS. WHITE RICE

- *Brown rice* is basically a whole grain, so it still has the bran, germ, and endosperm all intact. This rice not only has a little more texture, nuttiness, and chew but is also generally considered more nutritious.
- *White rice* is basically just the endosperm without the bran and germ.

Rice Cooker vs. Stovetop Method

I find that a rice cooker is the easiest and most carefree way to make perfectly cooked rice every time. You just set it and forget it, so if you have the space in your kitchen, I highly suggest getting one. That said, a rice cooker is definitely not essential and you can get equally amazing results on the stovetop with a little more TLC. Here's my stovetop method:

- *MEASURE* In a pot with a lid, measure out the amount of dry rice you want to cook (in general, 1 cup dry rice makes about 3 cups cooked rice).

- *RINSE* the rice (in the pot) under cool running water until the water runs clear. Rinsing the rice helps to remove excess starch and prevent the rice from getting gummy. Rinsing brown rice is usually pretty quick, while white rice can seem like it takes forever for the water to run clear—just do your best and then proceed to the next step.

- *DRAIN* the water as well as possible. For white rice, measure 1½ parts water to 1 part rice. For brown rice, measure 2 parts water to 1 part rice. For added flavor, you can substitute any type of liquid you want for the water (meat or vegetable stock, coconut water, unsweetened tea, etc.).

- **COOK** Bring the rice to a boil, then cover with the lid and reduce the heat to the lowest setting. Cook for 15 to 20 minutes for white rice and 35 to 40 minutes for brown rice. Turn the heat off and let the rice steam, covered, for 10 minutes. Fluff with a fork before serving.

Hot Sauces

I have an entire pantry shelf dedicated to just my hot sauces. I put hot sauce on everything, whether I'm cooking with it, drizzling it on food, or pouring it into my mouth because my tongue just loves the tingle. If you love a good mouth party, you'll know what I'm talking about. These hot sauces are *always* in my house:

1. *SAMBAL OELEK* Originally from Indonesia, this "chunky" hot sauce is made simply with crushed raw red chilies, vinegar, and salt. It's very versatile and has the "purest" flavor profile out there—making it delicious when used as a condiment or as an ingredient in cooking. If you can't find sambal oelek, you can also use chili garlic sauce as a perfect substitute in any of the recipes that call for it.

2. *CHOLULA* Thanks to the piquin and arbol chilies, this Mexican hot sauce is complexly flavored and has the perfect level of heat. It's hands down my favorite condiment for everyday use but happens to work really well as an ingredient in cooking too.

3. *XO SAUCE* This Chinese "hot sauce" is noticeably more expensive than the other ones on this list because it's made with dried shrimp and scallops (in addition to garlic, onions, chilies, and oil). It's worth every penny, and a little bit goes a long way. My favorite brand, which also happens to be the easiest to find, is Lee Kum Kee.

4. *SRIRACHA* Although sriracha is the sweetest of the bunch, it's also one of the spicier hot sauces in my pantry, so I like to use it with strong-flavored foods that won't get overpowered by the heat.

5. *TAPATÍO* Made without vinegar, this hot sauce tastes like a spicy salsa puree. It's one of the spicier sauces on this list and goes really well with food that doesn't need any additional acid but would benefit from some heat.

6. *LOUISIANA-STYLE HOT SAUCE* This hot sauce is one of the saltier but milder ones in the group. I usually use this when I'm not in the mood for too much heat, but still want a little pizzazz on my food.

7. *FRANK'S RED HOT* Most commonly used in recipes that call for buffalo sauce, this "buttery" hot sauce is one I always like to have in the pantry. Better to be safe than sorry because you just never know when you'll be in the mood for buffalo wings (which is surprisingly often for me).

Fats and Oils

Simply put, fat makes food taste better. It does this by evenly distributing the heat to food, whether you are roasting, sautéing, or frying, and assisting in the development of flavor, texture, and color. In general, different fats have different uses (which is not to say they can't be substituted in a pinch), so here is a list of the types I always have on hand:

TOASTED SESAME OIL

- No to low heat.
- Great for sauces, dressings, and drizzling.

EXTRA VIRGIN OLIVE OIL

- Low to medium-high heat.
- Great for sauces, dressings, drizzling, and sautéing (a.k.a. cooking something quickly in a pan with a little bit of fat over relatively high heat).

CANOLA OIL (OR SAFFLOWER OIL)

- Medium to very high heat.
- Great for searing, shallow-frying, stir-frying, deep-frying, and baking.

COOKING SPRAY

- I usually go for a neutral-flavored spray made with canola or avocado oil.
- Great for greasing a baking pan or getting even coverage on meats.

UNSALTED BUTTER

- This is the one fat that should be stored in the fridge. If a recipe calls for room temperature or softened butter, you can take it out a few hours before using or even leave it out overnight.
- Great for baking and adding flavor to savory dishes.

Soy Sauce

There are so many kinds of soy sauce that even I can get a little overwhelmed by them. In general, they are all made using fermented soybeans and wheat (don't come at me, all you soy sauce connoisseurs!). To keep things simple, I use an all-purpose reduced-sodium soy sauce as my go-to. I personally don't think it's necessary to have a different soy sauce for every different recipe, so test out a few types and see which is your favorite. The most important thing is to look for a soy sauce that has minimal ingredients consisting of mainly soybeans, wheat, salt, and water. And for anyone who is gluten-free, tamari is a great substitute for soy sauce (just double-check the label to be 100% sure).

Unseasoned Rice Vinegar

Rice vinegar is my favorite type of vinegar! It's made from fermented rice and is milder, sweeter, and less acidic than other types of vinegar. You generally find rice vinegar in two forms—seasoned and unseasoned. The difference is that seasoned rice vinegar has added sugar and salt, while the unseasoned one does not. I prefer the unseasoned variety since I can always just add my own sugar or salt if I want. Because the acid is lower in rice vinegar compared to other types of vinegar, it isn't ideal for preserving things, but aside from that, it's amazing for everything else! I use it for a quick pickle, salad dressings, and general seasoning for all types of dishes. Look for a brand that contains only rice and water. Lastly, if you are in a pinch, apple cider vinegar, white wine vinegar, or champagne vinegar can be substituted for rice vinegar.

Coconut Milk

Unsweetened full-fat coconut milk has so many uses that I always have a few cans of it in my pantry. Don't confuse full-fat coconut milk with low-fat coconut milk (which is simply watered down; if you need, you can water it down yourself), coconut cream (which is just coconut fat and will be too thick for most recipes), or cartons of coconut milk (which is sweetened and meant for drinking). Unsweetened, full-fat coconut milk is rich, incredibly versatile, and works in almost any recipe that calls for coconut milk. So, unless the recipe specifies otherwise, always reach for the unsweetened, full-fat kind.

Honey

I like to tell myself that honey is healthier than granulated sugar because it contains traces of vitamins and minerals, and busy little bees made it in their busy little bee house. In all seriousness though, I find honey to be pleasantly complex and it enhances the flavor of certain dishes in a more interesting way than regular sugar.

Garlic

I love fresh garlic and always have at least one head of it on my counter. I'm not a fan of the refrigerated minced garlic that comes in a jar, but I am admittedly obsessed with the minced garlic cubes that you find in the freezer section. If you see them at the store, stock up because they last forever in the freezer and will make your life so much easier.

Kosher Salt

Always use kosher salt because it's less briny than table salt and enhances the flavor of food versus making it just taste "salty" and metallic.

Freshly Ground Black Pepper

I'm sure you've heard this before, but I'm going to say it again. Freshly ground black pepper is always the better, brighter option than preground black pepper, which tends to have more of a muted flavor. The only type of preground pepper I use is ground white pepper, simply because whole white peppercorns aren't as readily available.

Fridge
Staples

Fish Sauce

At this point, you've probably eaten more fish sauce than you even know. Fish sauce is everywhere and in everything. It's salty, pungent, funky, and, some might even say, sweet. It adds a punch of unexplainable umami flavor that can transform a regular dish into a craveable dish. Small fish (such as anchovies) are covered in salt and then packed inside large barrels to ferment for anywhere from a couple of months to a couple of years, resulting in the beautiful savory liquid gold that we call fish sauce. When shopping for this all-in-one condiment, look for one that contains only fish and salt.

Yellow Miso Paste

Made from fermented soybeans, grains, salt, and koji (a type of mold), miso paste is another condiment that is salty, funky, and slightly sweet (but totally different than fish sauce). Since it's not as intense, miso paste is a great way to up the umami in a recipe without overpowering the other ingredients. Miso paste comes in a variety of colors: white is very mellow and sweet, yellow is salty and sweet, and red is very salty and intense. My go-to is a good quality yellow miso paste (make sure it's refrigerated and not the shelf-stable kind) because it's the perfect all-purpose miso and lasts for a really long time in the fridge.

Gochujang

Also known as Korean red chili paste, gochujang is one part salty, one part sweet, one part spicy, and entirely delicious. It's made from glutinous rice, fermented soybeans, salt, and sugar, resulting in a delicious, thick, sticky paste. You can use it in sauces or marinades, or to amp up flavor in a soup or stew. Every brand has a different heat level, so keep that in mind if you are using it for the first time.

Kimchi

Kimchi is a staple in Korean cuisine and is most commonly made with napa cabbage but can also be made with other kinds of vegetables, spices, and seasonings. I love kimchi for two main reasons. First, it's good for my gut health because it's fermented and, second, it's f*cking delicious. It goes well with everything because it's spicy, tangy, crunchy, and nutritious all in one perfect bite.

Parmigiano-Reggiano Cheese (or Parmesan)

I like to think of Parmigiano-Reggiano cheese as my little "flavor savior." If I ever make something that tastes a bit bland or needs a little pick-me-up, I'll add some grated or shaved Parmesan cheese to it, and all of a sudden, it's on a different level! I always have both a wedge and the pregrated in my fridge because no matter what happens, I know this cheese has my back.

Oyster Sauce

Oyster sauce has an indescribable sweet-and-salty flavor and is most often used in stir-fries and for seasoning steamed vegetables. The original oyster sauce was invented when Lee Kum Sheung, founder of the Lee Kum Kee brand, accidentally cooked a pot of oysters for far too long and ended up with a viscous, deep caramel–colored sauce that tasted surprisingly delicious. If only all my cooking accidents ended up as lucrative inventions of condiments! If you can find oyster sauce made from real oysters, definitely grab it, but there is absolutely nothing wrong with purchasing a brand that uses oyster extract as the first ingredient, as long as it has only a few other things in it (usually sugar and salt).

Tahini

To say that tahini is *just* ground sesame seeds is like saying Oprah is *just* a TV host. She is multifaceted, and so is tahini! To make tahini, sesame seeds are toasted before being ground into a slightly loose yet creamy, nutty, savory, and luxurious paste. Whether you're using it to make a dressing, sauce, or dip, make sure you find a brand that you like because not all tahini is created equal.

Natural Creamy Peanut Butter

Aside from being perfect for eating straight from the jar, natural peanut butter is also great for cooking and making sauces. I grew up eating the ultra-sweet, super-processed kind by the spoonful, but then I learned that it's not great for you or the environment, so I switched to natural peanut butter that's made with only peanuts and salt. At first, I was confused by the texture and top layer of oil, but I eventually discovered that the secret is to give the entire jar a good mix until it's nice and smooth. Then store it in the fridge, and it will be good to go from there on out.

Citrus

I always have an assortment of limes, lemons, and oranges in my fridge because they are extremely adaptable and have different levels of sweetness and acidity. The juice is perfect for things like freshening up a dish, making a dressing, or using in a drink, and the zest can be used as garnish and to add flavor as well.

Scallions

Also known as green onions, scallions are the easier-to-handle and more versatile sibling in the onion family. Scallions are a great way to add mild onion flavor without having to do much. They can be cooked or used raw as a garnish, and don't make you cry when you cut them up.

Ginger

I wasn't always a fan of ginger, but as my taste buds have developed over time, I find that this zingy root actually imparts a lot of subtle warmth to a dish. You may think of ginger as that pink pickled stuff you get with sushi, but that's not ginger in its original form. If you can't find fresh ginger, you can use frozen pregrated ginger or dried ground ginger.

Cilantro

You either love it or think it tastes like dish soap. If you happen to hate cilantro, you can omit this ingredient from any recipe that calls for it. The best way to keep cilantro fresh for as long as possible is to place the stems in a jar filled with a couple inches of water, loosely cover with an upside-down plastic bag, and place the jar in the fridge. Simply refresh the water every other day, and your cilantro should stay fresh for at least two weeks! This storage technique also works well for cut basil and parsley.

Sexy Sauces

SMOKY CHILI
Coconut Oil

Much like my husband at first glance (at least to me), this condiment looks hot and dangerous, but after one taste you learn that it's subtly sweet, emotionally available, and just spicy enough to keep things interesting. I understand the allure of the bad-boy chili oil that numbs your tongue, but I ultimately want a keeper that won't hurt me all the time or scare away my friends. Beautifully bright red, smoky, and texturally exciting, this chili oil goes well with so many things. Spoon it over scrambled, fried, or poached eggs. Stir-fry with some rice or noodles for a quick side dish. Drizzle it over grilled meats or all over Mama Woo's Pork & Shrimp Wontons (page 111). From the crunchy sesame seeds to the tamed Thai chilies giving off just the right amount of heat, you're about to get addicted to this sexy little number.

¼ cup coconut oil

¼ cup safflower or canola oil

4 cloves garlic, minced

3 Thai chilies or 1 serrano pepper, thinly sliced

1 tablespoon sesame seeds

1 tablespoon reduced-sodium soy sauce

1 tablespoon unseasoned rice vinegar

1 teaspoon granulated sugar

1 teaspoon smoked paprika

½ teaspoon ground cumin

MAKES ¼ CUP

In a small saucepan over medium-low heat, combine the coconut oil, safflower oil, garlic, chilies, sesame seeds, soy sauce, vinegar, sugar, paprika, and cumin. Cook until the mixture is fragrant and the chilies soften, 4 to 5 minutes, stirring constantly to prevent the garlic and spices from burning. Remove from the heat and let cool.

Storage

Use immediately or store in an airtight container (preferably a glass jar) in the fridge for up to 1 week. If the oil hardens in the fridge, just give it a good mix, scoop out what you need, and warm it up in a small saucepan before using.

*Everything
Sauce*
PAGE 29

*Garlicky
Almond &
Spinach
Pesto*
PAGE 28

*Smoky Chili
Coconut Oil*
PAGE 26

Garlicky
Almond
& Spinach
PESTO

There is always a surplus of nuts, leafy greens, Parmesan cheese, garlic, and olive oil in my house, so I find myself making a variation of pesto at least once a week. This is my favorite version, which is incredibly flavorful, versatile, and a great way to trick yourself into adding more greens to your diet. I like to use almonds instead of pine nuts because they are more readily available and I prefer the nuttier flavor. I also like my pesto with a lot of garlic, but feel free to play around with a little bit of this and a little bit of that to customize your pesto just the way you like. Toss it with some pasta or rice for a quick meal. Drizzle it all over scrambled, fried, or poached eggs. Spoon it over roasted steak, chicken, or fish. Dip your crudité or crackers into it. You can even dress a salad with it! Pesto really does have a million uses, but my favorite is Spicy Almond Pesto Udon with Baby Spinach & Burrata (page 106).

1 cup packed fresh regular or Thai basil (leaves and small stems)

½ cup packed baby spinach

¼ cup almonds, roasted and unsalted

6 cloves garlic, roughly chopped

½ cup extra virgin olive oil

½ cup grated Parmesan cheese

½ teaspoon kosher salt

½ teaspoon freshly ground black pepper

MAKES 1 CUP

In a food processor (or blender), combine the basil, spinach, almonds, garlic, oil, Parmesan, salt, and black pepper and blend until mostly smooth.

Storage

Store in an airtight container in the fridge for up to 5 days. You can also freeze it for up to 3 months (simply thaw in the fridge overnight and give it a quick stir before using).

Everything SAUCE

I use this sauce for everything (hence the name). It's salty, oniony, and garlicky, and it comes together incredibly quick. It also doubles as an all-purpose seasoning, which is why I always have a jar of it in my fridge. This sauce is perfect for stir-fries, fried rice, or fried noodles. You can use it to pump up the umami in your favorite soup or stew. It's absolutely delicious on steamed fish. Use it as a dipping sauce for dumplings or my Crab Cake Pot Stickers (page 141). It's so versatile and will transform whatever ingredients you have on hand into something you'll want to eat.

¼ cup reduced-sodium soy sauce

2 tablespoons unseasoned rice vinegar

2 teaspoons toasted sesame oil

1 teaspoon packed brown sugar (light or dark)

2 scallions, dark green parts only (about 1 tablespoon), minced

2 cloves garlic, minced

MAKES ½ CUP

In a small bowl, whisk together the soy sauce, vinegar, sesame oil, brown sugar, scallions, and garlic until the sugar dissolves.

Storage

Store in an airtight container in the fridge for up to 5 days.

SCALLION & BASIL *Chimichurri*

This bright and herbaceous extravaganza of a sauce is going to excite and delight your taste buds with reckless abandon. Since I like this sauce on the chunky side, I include the herb stems with the leaves because they add great body and texture. I prefer to chop all the herbs by hand, but if you want a smoother sauce, feel free to blitz everything in a food processor—it's going to be absolutely fantastic no matter how you make it. I suggest drizzling it on steak, chicken, fish, or vegetables, or using it as a marinade. It's also absolutely delicious as a salad dressing, served with crusty bread, or spooned over my Fugly Delicious Crispy Cheese Breakfast Tacos (page 49).

In a medium bowl, mix together the oil, vinegar, cilantro, parsley, basil, scallions, garlic, sugar, and salt until combined.

Storage

Store in an airtight container in the fridge for up to 5 days.

½ cup extra virgin olive oil

¼ cup unseasoned rice vinegar

½ cup packed fresh cilantro (leaves and small stems), finely chopped

¼ cup packed fresh flat-leaf parsley (leaves and small stems), finely chopped

¼ cup packed fresh basil (leaves and small stems), finely chopped

4 scallions, dark green parts only, finely chopped

2 cloves garlic, minced

½ teaspoon granulated sugar

1 teaspoon kosher salt

MAKES 1 CUP

*Spicy Peanut
Lime Sauce*
PAGE 32

*Spicy Sun-Dried
Tomato Pesto*
PAGE 33

*Scallion & Basil
Chimichurri*
PAGE 30

Spicy
Peanut Lime
SAUCE

You know something that *doesn't* go well with this spicy peanut lime sauce? No, seriously, I'm asking because I can't think of one thing. It's perfect on top of grilled chicken, salmon, or steak. You can serve it with crudité or toss it with shredded cabbage and carrots for a quick slaw. Try mixing it with some noodles or spreading it all over your sandwiches and burgers for a nutty twist. It can also be used as a dipping sauce for dumplings or my Sweet & Sticky Lamb Rib Chop "Satay" (page 239). When I make this particular sauce, I like to use an all-natural creamy peanut butter (the type that has only peanuts and salt) because I find the really processed options a little too sweet.

¼ cup unsweetened natural creamy peanut butter, stirred well

2 tablespoons fresh lime juice (about 1 lime)

1 tablespoon sambal oelek (more or less to taste)

2 teaspoons reduced-sodium soy sauce

1 teaspoon toasted sesame oil

1 teaspoon packed brown sugar

1 teaspoon grated fresh ginger

MAKES ½ CUP

In a small bowl, whisk together the peanut butter, lime juice, sambal oelek, soy sauce, sesame oil, brown sugar, ginger, and 2 to 3 tablespoons of water until smooth, adding more water as needed to reach your desired consistency. I like mine the consistency of honey so I can drizzle it over everything, but feel free to make it as thick or thin as you like.

Storage

Store in an airtight container in the fridge for up to 5 days.

Spicy Sun-Dried Tomato PESTO

Apparently sun-dried tomatoes were totally a thing in the food scene in the 1990s, but since I was just a tiny cherub-faced human and my brain was the size of a walnut at the time, I don't remember that. Honestly, though, trends come and go so fast I hardly remember what was cool last week! What I'm really trying to say is that I don't care what's cool at any given moment (especially in the food world) because I like what I like. Whether you think sun-dried tomatoes are hip or not doesn't really matter because this sauce will always have a place in my heart. The sun-dried tomatoes bring acid, sweetness, and so much umami, while the walnuts and Parmesan balance it out. Try spooning it over sliced fresh mozzarella, tossing it with some pasta, or dipping crusty bread into it. You can even serve it with some raw or cooked vegetables or, better yet, swirl it into my Cacio e Pepe Cauliflower "Polenta" (page 172) for an extra flavor punch! There is just so much goodness packed into this beautiful, flexible sauce that it's going to lovingly smack you in the face and you're going to like it.

½ cup extra virgin olive oil, plus more as needed

¼ cup sun-dried tomatoes (from a jar packed in olive oil), roughly chopped

¼ cup walnuts, roasted and unsalted, roughly chopped

2 tablespoons grated Parmesan cheese

1 teaspoon crushed red pepper flakes (optional)

¼ teaspoon freshly ground black pepper

2 cloves garlic, roughly chopped

MAKES 1 CUP

In a food processor (or blender), combine the oil, sun-dried tomatoes, walnuts, Parmesan, pepper flakes (if using), black pepper, and garlic and blend until smooth, adding more oil as necessary to help everything come together. Scrape down the sides with a silicone spatula and pulse a few more times until the sauce has an even consistency.

Storage

Store in an airtight container in the fridge for up to 5 days. You can also freeze for up to 3 months (simply thaw in the fridge overnight and give it a quick stir before using).

Crunchy Corn
Onion Dip
PAGE 36

Bibimbap-
Style Sauce
PAGE 35

Quick Spicy
Mayo
PAGE 37

Bibimbap-Style SAUCE

This is my take on one of my absolute favorite sauces in the entire galaxy. It's a little spicy, a touch creamy, and a whole lot of delicious. This sauce is typically served with bibimbap (go figure!), a bomb-ass Korean rice bowl topped with various veggies, grilled meat, and a fried egg, and—personally—I think it's the star of the dish. My version is less traditional because I add a bit of tahini to the mix, which makes the sauce just a little nutty and a little luxurious. This brightly colored sauce goes perfectly with my Bulgogi Pork Tenderloin Lettuce Wraps (page 236), but it's so f*cking delicious that I end up putting it on everything within arm's reach (like eggs, rice, roasted meats, and vegetables).

2 tablespoons gochujang

1 tablespoon tahini

2 teaspoons unseasoned rice vinegar

1 clove garlic, minced

MAKES ¼ CUP

In a small bowl, whisk together the gochujang, tahini, vinegar, garlic, and 2 tablespoons of water until smooth (preferably the consistency of honey), adding more water as needed.

Storage

Store in an airtight container in the fridge for up to 5 days.

CRUNCHY CORN
Onion Dip

This crunchy creation is a mix between an onion dip and a tzatziki (but instead of cucumbers, I use fresh corn). This is the only time I'll say that you *have* to use fresh corn because that juicy crunch and fresh sweetness are what take this dip to an entirely different level. Parmesan cheese gives it an umami punch, while the lemon brightens everything up. As a sauce, serve it alongside your favorite grilled meats or dolloped on top of tacos. As a dip, use it for crudité, potato chips, or my Crispy Hot Honey Baked Chicken Wings (page 133). However you decide to serve this, you'll find it's so refreshingly addictive that you might just end up eating it naked with only a spoon.

In a medium bowl, mix together the yogurt, corn kernels, Parmesan, lemon juice, oil, onion powder, garlic powder, hot sauce, dill, salt, and black pepper until combined.

Storage

Store in an airtight container in the fridge for up to 3 days.

1 cup plain whole or 2% Greek yogurt

½ cup freshly cut sweet corn kernels (from about 1 ear corn)

¼ cup grated Parmesan cheese

2 tablespoons fresh lemon juice

2 tablespoons extra virgin olive oil

1 teaspoon onion powder

1 teaspoon garlic powder

1 teaspoon hot sauce (I prefer Cholula)

½ teaspoon dried dill

½ teaspoon kosher salt

½ teaspoon freshly ground black pepper

MAKES 1½ CUPS

QUICK
Spicy Mayo

What does it even *mean* when someone says, "I don't really like mayo"? My mind refuses to register such a ridiculous statement because everyone already eats a buttload of eggs, oil, and vinegar, but when you combine these things to make an irresistibly luscious spread, it's all of a sudden gross? No, I do not accept. I love mayonnaise, and the only thing better than plain mayo is one that's spicy. Use this quick spicy mayo to spread on your sandwiches and burgers for a subtle kick, or try it as a dipping sauce for your fries, potato chips, or pot stickers. It also happens to go wonderfully with my Ahi Tuna & Salmon Poke Bowls with Brown Sushi Rice (page 214).

¼ cup mayonnaise or Kewpie Japanese mayonnaise

1 tablespoon sriracha or sambal oelek

1 teaspoon toasted sesame oil

½ teaspoon reduced-sodium soy sauce

MAKES ¼ CUP

In a small bowl, whisk together the mayonnaise, sriracha, sesame oil, and soy sauce until combined.

Storage

Store in an airtight container in the fridge for up to 5 days.

Breakfast All Day, Err'Day

Cheesy Chili Oil Egg Sandwich 40 • Fluffy Baked Vanilla Soufflé Pancakes 43
• Kimchi & Italian Sausage Fried Rice with Poached Eggs 46 • Fugly Delicious
Crispy Cheese Breakfast Tacos 49 • Crispy-Spicy-Vinegary Egg Omelet 50 •
Savory Cheddar Steel-Cut Oats with Chicken Apple Sausage, Avocado & Spinach
53 • Not-Too-Sweet Coconut, Quinoa & Goji Berry Granola 54 • Teriyaki Rib Eye
& Caramelized Onion Grilled Cheese 57 • Iced Matcha Latte with Watermelon
& Boba 58 • Cha Siu Bacon & Crispy Fried Eggs 60 • One Big-Ass Buttermilk
Cinnamon Roll 63

CHEESY CHILI OIL
Egg Sandwich

2 large brioche
    hamburger buns

2 tablespoons
    mayonnaise, plus
    more for serving

6 large eggs

½ cup finely
    shredded
    cheese, any kind

2 tablespoons chili
    oil

2 slices American
    cheese

Hot sauce, for
    serving

SERVES 2

I go through eggs faster than you can say cock-a-doodle-doo. In fact, I even considered raising a squad of chickens in my backyard before I quickly realized they would drive our dogs berserk (and it's way less work to just buy eggs at the store). Eggs can be turned into virtually anything your heart desires, and my little heart wants these deliciously cheesy egg sandwiches all the time. They are super quick to make and undeniably satisfying. It's really hard to go wrong with cheesy, creamy soft-scrambled eggs snuggled in between buttery, fluffy toasted brioche buns. Speaking of, make sure to use the softest buns you can get your hands on because that's how you'll get the perfect egg-to-carb ratio in every bite.

Toast the Buns	Heat a large nonstick skillet over medium-low heat and evenly spread ½ tablespoon of mayonnaise on each cut side of the buns. Place the buns cut side down onto the hot skillet and cook until toasted and golden brown, 2 to 3 minutes. Brioche bread burns really fast, so make sure to keep your eyes on it. Transfer to a plate and set aside.
Cook the Eggs	In a medium bowl, whisk together the eggs and shredded cheese until combined. In the same nonstick skillet used to toast the buns, heat the chili oil on low heat. When the oil is warm, add the egg mixture. Now here is the important part: using a silicone spatula, scrape down the sides of the skillet and push the eggs toward the center while also scraping all over the bottom. The key is to make sure the eggs are not in contact with the pan for too long so they don't get rubbery. Yes, you have to do this for an entire 5 minutes (it's not that long!), so don't be tempted to crank up the heat. (If your eggs begin to brown even a little, immediately remove the pan from the heat, but as long as you keep the heat on low, you shouldn't run into this issue.) When the eggs are almost done (they should still look wet and shiny), use your spatula to form two "egg patties" (each about the same size as the buns) and top each patty with a slice of American cheese. Turn the heat off and leave the skillet on the burner until the cheese has slightly melted, 30 to 60 seconds.

➜

| Whip the Egg Whites | In a clean, dry bowl of a stand mixer fitted with the whisk attachment (or using a hand mixer), whip the egg whites, vinegar, and vanilla on high speed until stiff peaks form, about 1 minute. When you lift the whisk attachment, the peaks should stand straight up. Using a silicone spatula, gently fold the whipped egg whites into the egg yolk mixture until just combined and no streaks remain (again, don't overmix!), making sure to scrape down the sides and bottom of the bowl. |

| Bake the Pancakes | Divide the batter between the prepared ramekins and place on a baking sheet. Transfer to the oven and immediately reduce the oven temperature to 375°F. Bake until puffed up and browned on top, 18 to 20 minutes. To check if they are done, insert a toothpick into the center, and if it comes out clean, you are good to go! Dust with powdered sugar and serve warm with butter and maple syrup. |

Make Ahead

Unlike actual soufflés (which can be finicky), these soufflé pancakes can be made in advance (without the powdered sugar and syrup), covered in plastic wrap, and stored in the fridge for up to 2 days. When you are ready to eat, nuke them in the microwave for 30 to 60 seconds until warm.

Kimchi & Italian Sausage
FRIED RICE
with Poached Eggs

4 large eggs

1 tablespoon distilled white vinegar or rice vinegar

Kosher salt

Freshly ground black pepper

2 tablespoons unsalted butter

½ small onion, finely chopped

½ pound uncooked Italian sausage (sweet or spicy) or breakfast sausage, casing removed

½ cup kimchi, finely chopped

2 cups cooked short-grain rice (white or brown), preferably day-old

1 teaspoon toasted sesame oil

SERVES 4

If you don't eat rice in the morning, you really need to start living your best life. Rice is perfect for any time of day and, in my opinion, especially breakfast. I love making this "breakfast" fried rice because I don't have to wait until dinnertime to eat it—although it is also perfect for dinner . . . or lunch or even a midnight snack (and who doesn't love a good midnight snack?). It's laced with hearty Italian sausage and little bits of tangy kimchi and topped with a delicately poached egg. The runny yolk, which is pure liquid gold, melts into the rice and ties everything together—making this dish pure perfection.

| Poach the Eggs | Line a plate with a paper towel and set aside. Bring a large pot of water to a rolling boil, then reduce the heat to the lowest setting. Place a fine-mesh sieve over a small bowl and crack one egg into it. The watery parts of the egg whites will strain through, while the thicker part of the egg whites will stay in the sieve with the yolk. Transfer the strained egg to another small bowl, discarding the strained whites. Add the vinegar to the water and, using a spoon, stir the water to create a vortex. Gently slide the egg into the center of the vortex and cook until the whites are just set but the yolk is still runny, about 3 minutes. Remove the poached egg with a slotted spoon and transfer to the paper towel–lined plate. Repeat with the remaining eggs. Season the poached eggs with salt and black pepper and set aside while you make the fried rice. |

| Cook the Sausage | In a large skillet or wok over medium heat, melt the butter. When the butter has melted, add the onion and cook until translucent and the edges begin to brown, 4 to 6 minutes. Add the sausage and cook until browned, 5 to 6 minutes, breaking up any large chunks. Stir in the kimchi and cook until just hot, 2 to 3 minutes. |

| Finish the Dish | Stir in the rice and sesame oil, breaking up any large chunks of rice. Spread the rice into an even layer and cook, undisturbed, until crispy on the bottom, 2 to 3 minutes. Transfer to a serving dish, top with the poached eggs, and serve hot. |

Fugly Delicious Crispy Cheese
BREAKFAST TACOS

2 cups shredded Cheddar cheese (mild or sharp)

4 large eggs

Chili powder

Freshly ground black pepper

1 medium avocado, diced

4 slices bacon, cooked to your preference, roughly chopped

Sour cream, for serving

Scallion & Basil Chimichurri (page 30), for serving

Hot sauce, for serving

SERVES 2

Believe it or not, there are days when I crave a taco *without* the tortilla. The thing is that a taco isn't a taco without a shell, so I still need *something* to wrap everything up! Since I just happen to be *that* person who loves cheese so much that I'll pile it onto a plate and microwave it just so I can satisfy my craving for warm melty cheese, it only made sense that I created a taco "shell" entirely out of this magical dairy product. My mission was to make a carb-less taco, but what I ended up with was something more satisfying and fun to eat than I could have ever imagined. Since the cheese and the egg are cooked at the same time, the edges of the slowly melting cheese crisp up while the egg cooks to runny yolk perfection. Right before shoving this beauty into my mouth, I like to drizzle my Scallion & Basil Chimichurri sauce (page 30) all over it because it has just the right amount of acidity to cut the fattiness of the cheese and bacon. Now, depending on who you ask, it's either fugly delicious or beautiful delicious, but either way you will think it's just freaking delicious.

Make the Taco "Shell"

On a large nonstick griddle or skillet over medium heat, take ½ cup of shredded Cheddar and make a 5-inch-wide nest, repeating with the rest of the cheese and fitting as many as you can onto the hot surface (you may have to make these in batches). Crack an egg into the middle of each "cheese nest" and season with chili powder and black pepper to taste. Cook until the cheese is browned on the edges and the whites of the eggs are set (but the yolks are still runny), 6 to 7 minutes.

Add the Toppings

Transfer to a serving plate and top with the avocado, bacon, sour cream, chimichurri, and hot sauce. Fold in half and eat your face off.

Crispy-Spicy-Vinegary

EGG OMELET

1 tablespoon fish
sauce

1 teaspoon
granulated
sugar

1 teaspoon
unseasoned rice
vinegar

1 teaspoon sambal
oelek, plus more
for serving

4 large eggs

1 tablespoon
rice flour or
cornstarch

2 scallions, dark
green parts only,
finely chopped

¼ cup canola oil or
any other high-
heat oil

2 cups cooked rice,
for serving

2 tablespoons
finely chopped
cilantro, for
garnish

SERVES 2

The first time I visited Thailand (many moons ago), I became obsessed with something called khai jiao. It's a Thai egg dish that's surprisingly light and easy to make yet deeply satisfying. It also happens to be crispy, vinegary, and spicy—I mean, what's not to love? Much like my face, this might look like a plain, overly browned omelet, but like I always say, never judge something until you put it in your mouth (this applies only to food, people!). The textures are a combination of crackly and tender, and the flavors give you tongue tingles in the best way possible. Also, did I mention you can have all of this delicious excitement in just a matter of minutes?

Prep the Sauce & Eggs

In a small bowl, whisk together the fish sauce, sugar, vinegar, sambal oelek, and 1 tablespoon of water until the sugar dissolves. In a large bowl, whisk together the eggs, rice flour, scallions, and 1 tablespoon of the prepared sauce until light and frothy.

Cook the Eggs

Line a plate with two layers of paper towels and set aside. In a medium nonstick skillet over high heat, add the oil. When the oil is hot, evenly (and carefully) pour half of the frothy eggs into the pan and cook, undisturbed, until the edges are golden brown and crispy (the center will still be kind of wet), 45 to 60 seconds. Using a silicone spatula, carefully flip the omelet (don't worry if it becomes a little misshapen) and cook until the center is set, 45 to 60 more seconds. Transfer the omelet to the paper towel–lined plate and repeat with the remaining egg mixture.

Serve

Divide the rice among two plates. Top each with an omelet and a spoonful of the remaining sauce. Garnish with cilantro and serve with sambal oelek.

Tip

I know this recipe calls for what seems like a lot of oil, but we are essentially shallow-frying the eggs to get those crispy edges. Don't worry, most of the oil will get soaked up by the paper towel.

Steel-Cut Oats

with Chicken Apple Sausage, Avocado & Spinach

½ cup steel-cut oats

2 cups water or chicken stock

1 cup milk (whole or low-fat)

½ teaspoon kosher salt, plus more for the spinach

2 tablespoons unsalted butter

¼ cup shredded sharp Cheddar cheese

2 tablespoons grated Parmesan cheese

2 tablespoons extra virgin olive oil

2 links fully cooked chicken apple sausage, sliced

5 ounces baby spinach

Freshly ground black pepper

1 avocado, diced

Chili oil, for drizzling

SERVES 2

This recipe is a shout-out to my dad because he was actually the one who introduced me to the idea of savory oats. Don't get me wrong: I still love me some sweet-ass oatmeal, but after discovering all the possibilities of a savory version, the two kinds are now officially tied for the title of Coziest Breakfast Food. Although you can really use any type of oatmeal for this recipe, I like nutty, chewy steel-cut oats. They take a little longer to cook, but it's worth it because when they're done you end up with something that's even more toothsome and hearty than a big, warm bowl of cheesy breakfast grits (don't knock it till you try it!). I like to top mine with pieces of sweet chicken apple sausage, hearty chunks of creamy avocado, and some wilted spinach, but feel free to use whatever toppings you want to make it your own.

Cook the Oats

In a medium pot, combine the oats, water, milk, and salt and bring to a boil (keep an eye on it as the milk will bubble up very fast). Immediately reduce the heat to a simmer and cook until the oats are tender and resemble porridge, 25 to 30 minutes, stirring occasionally. Stir in the butter and cheeses. If the oatmeal gets too thick, add a little more milk or water to loosen it up. Remove from the heat and cover while you cook the sausage and spinach.

Cook the Sausage & Spinach

In a medium skillet over medium heat, add the oil and sausage. Cook until the sausage is browned and warmed through, 2 to 3 minutes on each side. Transfer the sausages to a plate and set aside. Add the spinach to the skillet and season with salt and black pepper. Cook until just wilted, about 1 minute.

Serve

Divide the cooked oats between two bowls and top with the cooked sausage and spinach. Garnish with avocado chunks and chili oil. Serve warm.

NOT-TOO-SWEET
Coconut, Quinoa & Goji Berry
GRANOLA

¼ cup pineapple juice

¼ cup honey or maple syrup

2 tablespoons packed brown sugar (light or dark)

2 tablespoons canola oil

1½ cups old-fashioned rolled oats

½ cup dried goji berries

½ cup slivered almonds

½ cup unsweetened coconut flakes

½ cup quinoa, any color, rinsed and drained

2 teaspoons pure vanilla extract

1 teaspoon ground cinnamon

½ teaspoon kosher salt

Greek yogurt, any flavor, for serving

Mandarins, peeled and sliced, for serving

SERVES 6

There's always some variation of homemade granola on our kitchen counter because Doug and I love this stuff almost as much as we love each other. And out of all the granola recipes I make, this is our favorite—and the most versatile. It's lightly sweetened with pineapple juice, honey, and just a kiss of brown sugar, so it's not cloying like the store-bought stuff. Mama Woo has been cooking with goji berries for decades now, and I love adding them to my granola (but feel free to substitute dried cranberries or raisins). For added crunch, I throw in some slivered almonds, but again, feel free to substitute whatever kind of nut you like. Aside from all the customization, the best thing about this recipe is that you can serve it in so many different ways. Whether it's simply with some cold milk, as a crunchy topping on a salad, or with Greek yogurt and slices of juicy mandarin (my personal go-to), you're going to love this granola as much as we do.

Mix the Ingredients	Position a rack in the center of the oven and preheat the oven to 300°F. Line a baking sheet with parchment paper. In a large bowl, whisk together the pineapple juice, honey, brown sugar, and oil until the sugar dissolves. Add the oats, goji berries, almonds, coconut flakes, quinoa, vanilla, cinnamon, and salt and use a silicone spatula to stir everything together until thoroughly mixed, scraping down the sides and bottom of the bowl.
Bake the Granola	Spread the mixture in an even layer on the prepared baking sheet and bake until golden brown, 40 to 45 minutes, tossing halfway through. Do not be tempted to cook it any longer or the goji berries will burn. The mixture will feel moist to the touch straight out of the oven but will crisp up as it cools.
Serve	Let the granola cool completely and serve with Greek yogurt and sliced mandarins.
Storage	Once the granola is completely cooled, store in an airtight container or freezer bag at room temperature for up to 5 days.

TERIYAKI RIB EYE
& *Caramelized Onion* GRILLED CHEESE

2 tablespoons reduced-sodium soy sauce

1 teaspoon packed brown sugar (light or dark)

1 clove garlic, minced

¼ teaspoon freshly ground black pepper

1 tablespoon canola oil

1 pound boneless rib eye steak, thinly sliced against the grain

Kosher salt

Freshly ground black pepper

½ medium onion, thinly sliced

4 teaspoons mayonnaise

4 slices sourdough, buttermilk, or your favorite white bread

4 slices sharp Cheddar cheese or American cheese

SERVES 2

You know that moment when you wake up in the morning refreshed, bursting with energy, and ready to take on the day? Yeah, me neither. I am admittedly NOT a morning person, and sometimes I need help getting out of bed—whether that's my husband dragging me out, my dogs stomping all over my boy parts, or a truly motivating breakfast. And by "motivating," I mean something so satisfying and worthwhile that I'm practically jumping out of my warm, cozy bed for it. THIS is that motivational breakfast. Meaty, fatty, and juicy ribeye steak paired with the natural sweetness of caramelized onions and a quick teriyaki sauce makes this grilled cheese sandwich a breakfast fit for a king (or queen)—and I'm a royal, goddammit!

Make the Sauce

In a small bowl, whisk together the soy sauce, brown sugar, garlic, and black pepper until the sugar dissolves. Set aside.

Cook the Steak & Onions

In a large cast-iron skillet over high heat, add the oil. When the oil is hot, add the sliced steak and season with salt and black pepper. Cook until the steak is browned, about 1 minute on each side, making sure none of the slices stick together. Transfer the steak to a plate and set aside. To the same skillet, add the onion and cook until translucent and slightly charred, 4 to 5 minutes, tossing often. Add the cooked steak back into the skillet along with the prepared sauce and cook until the sauce thickens, about 30 seconds, tossing continuously. Remove from the heat.

Assemble the Sandwich

Spread 1 teaspoon of mayonnaise edge to edge on one side of each slice of bread. On a nonstick griddle over medium-low heat, place the bread mayonnaise side down, top each with a slice of cheese, and cook until the bread is golden brown on the bottom and the cheese is melted, 6 to 7 minutes. (Toasting the bread on relatively low heat helps to minimize the risk of burning the bread while giving the cheese time to melt.) Divide the cooked steak and onions between two slices of bread and invert the other two slices on top. Plate them up and get ready to become happy morning people.

Tip

To get super-thin slices of steak, pop that rib eye in the freezer for a couple of hours to firm up just before slicing. If you don't have the patience for that, just slice the steak as thinly as you can straight out of the fridge (the sharper the knife, the better).

ICED
Matcha Latte
with Watermelon & Boba

½ cup uncooked quick-cooking boba (tapioca pearls)

¾ cup very finely diced watermelon (small enough to fit through a boba straw)

2 teaspoons matcha (green tea powder)

1 cup cold milk

¼ cup sweetened condensed milk (optional)

SERVES 2

Tip
Quick-cooking boba can be found at most Asian grocery stores or online.

There is only one person who loves boba more than I do and that's my oldest sister, Melissa. Every time I go to her house, she's sipping on a boba drink, always with a double scoop of boba (a.k.a. tapioca pearls) and tiny bits of fresh fruit. And because she always looks so happy with her drink, I end up craving this sweet treat as well! It's a vicious (but delicious) cycle that we just can't quit. I put this drink in the breakfast chapter because the matcha has caffeine in it, but the truth is that this refreshment-snack hybrid is really an any-time-of-the-day kind of thing. You can make it for breakfast or drink it with your lunch. It's great as an afternoon snack by the pool or even at dinnertime. (May I suggest that you pair it with just about *anything* from this book?) What I'm basically saying is that there's never a wrong time for a creamy iced matcha latte filled with chewy tapioca pearls and niblets of juicy watermelon.

Cook the Boba — Cook the boba according to the package directions. Rinse with cold running water, drain, and divide between two large glasses. Top with the diced watermelon.

Make the Matcha Latte — Bring 1 cup of water to a boil, then immediately turn the heat off and let sit for 2 minutes. In a blender, combine the hot water and the matcha and blend on high speed until frothy, 30 to 45 seconds. Add the cold milk and continue blending until it's even frothier, 30 to 45 seconds.

Assemble the Drink — Top off each glass with ice followed by the blended matcha. Spoon the condensed milk (if using) on top and give everything a quick stir before enjoying!

CHA SIU BACON
& Crispy Fried Eggs

½ cup pineapple juice

¼ cup ketchup

2 tablespoons packed brown sugar (light or dark)

2 tablespoons reduced-sodium soy sauce

1 tablespoon sriracha (optional)

3 cloves garlic, minced

1 pound pork butt or shoulder, cut into ¼-inch slices

2 tablespoons extra virgin olive oil

4 large eggs

2 cups cooked short-grain rice (white or brown), for serving

Toasted sesame seeds, for garnish

SERVES 4

You know how some people say the best things in life are free? Well, they're wrong because cha siu (a.k.a. Chinese barbecued pork) is one of the best things in life, and the last time I checked, it wasn't free. Cha siu can usually be found at any good Chinese restaurant or Asian barbecue meat shop and most often comes in the form of thick strips of pork butt covered in a shiny red glaze that's as beautiful as it is scrumptious. And although cha siu isn't free, it's not expensive to make either! In my version, the pork butt is sliced before getting marinated overnight in a salty-sweet mixture, resulting in individual pieces of cha siu that are intensely flavored on every side. Tender, fatty, and irresistible—all you need now is a bowl of warm rice and some crispy fried eggs.

Marinate the Pork Butt

In a small bowl, whisk together the pineapple juice, ketchup, brown sugar, soy sauce, sriracha (if using), and garlic until the sugar dissolves. Transfer the mixture to a freezer bag along with the pork and massage the marinade into each slice, making sure every piece is coated. Squeeze out as much air as possible, seal, and refrigerate for at least 6 hours (or up to 2 days in advance).

Cook the Pork Butt

Remove the slices of pork from the marinade and arrange in an even layer in a large nonstick skillet. Discard the remaining marinade. Add 1 cup of water to the skillet, set to medium-high heat, and cook until the water evaporates, 10 to 12 minutes. Reduce the heat to medium-low and flip the pork pieces. Cook until they are browned and caramelized, 3 to 4 minutes on each side, adjusting the heat as needed to prevent burning (a little char is fine). Transfer the pork to a plate and clean the skillet.

Cook the Eggs

In the clean skillet over medium heat, add the olive oil. When the oil is hot, crack the eggs into the skillet and fry until the edges are crispy, the whites are set, but the yolks are still runny, about 2 minutes.

Serve

Divide the cooked rice among four plates. Top each with the char siu bacon, a sprinkle of sesame seeds, and a fried egg. Serve immediately.

Did You Eat Yet?

One Big-Ass BUTTERMILK Cinnamon Roll

This recipe is one of my most prized creations because (a) it does not require yeast, which means no proofing time, (b) the entire thing tastes like the ooey-gooey center part of a Cinnabon, and (c) it is a f*cking showstopper. If you didn't already guess from the name, it's not a regular cinnamon roll; it's a *big-ass* one. When this beauty comes out of the oven, the melted butter gets absorbed back into the roll, and by frosting it while it's hot, all that sweet cream-cheese goodness oozes into the cracks and crevices, resulting in the most glorious pie-size cinnamon roll you have ever seen. I promise you that this big boy will hit the spot all morning long until your eyes roll to the back of your head. And let's be honest, that sounds like a pretty good way to start the day.

DOUGH

1¼ cups all-purpose flour, plus more for dusting

1 tablespoon granulated sugar

1½ teaspoons baking powder

½ teaspoon baking soda

¼ teaspoon kosher salt

½ cup buttermilk

2 tablespoons unsalted butter, melted

1 large egg

FILLING

8 tablespoons (1 stick) unsalted butter, softened

½ cup packed brown sugar (light or dark)

2 tablespoons ground cinnamon

¼ teaspoon kosher salt

CREAM CHEESE FROSTING

1 cup powdered sugar

4 ounces (½ brick) cream cheese, room temperature

2 tablespoons unsalted butter, softened

1 teaspoon pure vanilla extract or maple syrup

SERVES 6

Make Ahead

To save time, the dough can be made the night before, covered in plastic wrap, and stored in the fridge until you're ready to bake the next morning. The filling and frosting can also be made the night before, covered with plastic wrap, and stored at room temperature.

In the Mood for a More "Classic" Big-Ass Cinnamon Roll?

Swap the dough in this recipe for the yeasted dough in the bao recipe (page 151). Simply make the yeasted dough (as directed in the bao recipe), and then proceed with the directions to the right for filling, assembly, baking, and frosting.

Make the Dough

Position a rack in the center of the oven and preheat the oven to 350°F. Line a 9-inch pie dish with parchment paper (with ample overhang) and set aside. In a large bowl, whisk together the flour, sugar, baking powder, baking soda, and salt. Create a well in the center of the dry ingredients and add the buttermilk, melted butter, and egg. Starting from the middle, use a wooden spoon (or silicone spatula) to mix the ingredients in a circular motion, slowly working your way to the sides of the bowl. The dough will be very soft and pretty sticky. Scrape down the sides of the bowl and roughly shape the dough into a ball. Let the dough rest in the fridge, uncovered, for about 30 minutes while you make the filling and the frosting.

Make the Filling

In a small bowl, mix together the softened butter, brown sugar, cinnamon, and salt until combined. Set aside.

Make the Frosting

In a medium bowl, add the powdered sugar, cream cheese, butter, and vanilla. Using an electric hand mixer fitted with the whisk attachment, beat on low speed until crumbly, about 30 seconds. Increase the speed to high and beat until smooth, about 2 minutes. Set aside.

Assemble the Cinnamon Roll

Scrape the dough out onto a well-floured surface and sprinkle more flour on top of it. Use your hands to gently stretch and shape the dough into a 1-inch-thick log (it will be about 2½ feet long). Continue dusting with flour as needed in order to easily handle the dough. Use a rolling pin to gently flatten the dough into a 3-inch-wide strip (the length of the log doesn't matter as much as the width). Spread half of the filling onto the strip and fold in half lengthwise to make a 1½-inch wide strip (gently flatten it out if needed). Spread the remaining filling on top of the strip and, starting from one end, carefully roll into a cinnamon roll.

Bake the Cinnamon Roll

Carefully transfer the roll to the center of the prepared pie dish and bake until it is just barely brown (but not *too* brown or it will be dry), 22 to 26 minutes. As soon as the cinnamon roll comes out of the oven, spread the frosting all over the top so it can melt into the crevices. Let the cinnamon roll cool for 5 minutes before serving warm. Any leftovers should be tightly covered in plastic wrap and kept at room temperature; they are best eaten within a day.

How to Assemble the Cinnamon Roll

step 1	step 2

step 3	step 4

step 5	step 6

step 7	step 8	step 9

Healthy Ish

Little Gem & Citrus Salad with Feta & Creamy Lime Dressing 68 • Endive & Arugula Salad with Asian Pear & Goat Cheese 71 • Napa Cabbage & Spinach Chopped Salad with Lemony Basil Dressing 72 • Kale & Carrot Salad with Miso-Mustard Dressing 74 • Hawaiian Chicken Vermicelli Bowl 76 • Easy Golden Egg Fried Rice 78 • Mama Woo's Minced Beef & Rice Bowls 81 • "Creamy" Hot & Sour Turkey Soup with Spinach & Egg 82 • Chunky Corn & Sweet Potato Chowder 84 • Turkey & Mushroom Collard Green Wraps with Crunchy Peanuts 87 • Spicy Coconut Curry Chickpea & Cherry Tomato Stew 88

LITTLE GEM &
Citrus Salad
with Feta & Creamy Lime Dressing

You know when you have a potluck with your friends and you're assigned the salad, while basic Amy gets to make the party-favorite cheesy pasta dish? Everyone ends up forgetting about your contribution, and she gets to bask in all the praise. Not today, Satan! I promise you this will NOT happen if you bring *this* salad full of crunchy gem lettuce, sweet and juicy orange segments, briny chunks of feta, and a creamy-tangy lime dressing. Everybody will *actually* want to eat this (as opposed to feeling obligated). Not only does this salad travel well, but because the lettuce is cut into hefty wedges, you can eat it with a fork and knife—which also makes it feel more substantial. And after this gorgeous salad has been gobbled up, the only thing left will be Amy's soggy-ass macaroni casserole (unless she made my Red Curry Mac 'n' Cheese from page 101, then all bets are off).

2 tablespoons fresh lime juice

2 tablespoons mayonnaise

2 tablespoons grated Parmesan cheese

2 teaspoons Dijon mustard

1 clove garlic, minced

¼ teaspoon kosher salt

¼ teaspoon freshly ground black pepper

¼ cup extra virgin olive oil

4 heads Little Gem lettuce, quartered lengthwise (or 1 head romaine, cut into 8 wedges lengthwise)

2 navel, blood, or Cara Cara oranges, peeled and segmented

2 ounces feta cheese, cut into ½-inch cubes

¼ cup fresh flat-leaf parsley, roughly chopped

Lime wedges, for serving

SERVES 2

Make the Dressing

In a small bowl, whisk together the lime juice, mayonnaise, Parmesan, mustard, garlic, salt, and black pepper until smooth. Continue whisking as you drizzle in the olive oil until thoroughly emulsified. Refrigerate until ready to use. The dressing will keep in an airtight container in the fridge for up to 3 days.

Assemble the Salad

Arrange the gem lettuce on a large serving dish. Drizzle half of the dressing on top, adding more as needed. Top with orange segments, feta, and parsley. Serve with lime wedges and the remaining dressing on the side.

ENDIVE & ARUGULA *Salad* with

Asian Pear & Goat Cheese

3 tablespoons fresh orange juice

1 tablespoon red wine vinegar

1 tablespoon Dijon mustard

¼ cup extra virgin olive oil

½ shallot, finely chopped

Kosher salt

Freshly ground black pepper

3 heads endive, quartered lengthwise

2 cups baby arugula

1 small Asian pear, very thinly sliced

2 ounces goat cheese, crumbled

¼ cup roasted sliced almonds

SERVES 2

Asian pears are my spirit fruit (kind of like a spirit animal, but produce) and are the unsung heroes of the fruit world. They're everything you could possibly want in a fruit—sweet, crunchy, and juicy—but for some reason don't get nearly the amount of attention that they deserve. Not only are they the bomb.com for snacking as is, they play well in savory dishes too. This salad is simple to make, looks gorgeous, and gives me all the right (mouth) feels. Everything from the subtle tanginess of the orange vinaigrette to the bitter endive to the peppery arugula to the salty goat cheese to the crunchy almonds and, of course, the Asian pears (I pretty much just listed all the ingredients, folks!) makes this a perfectly well-balanced salad.

Make the Vinaigrette

In a small bowl, whisk together the orange juice, vinegar, and mustard until smooth. Continue whisking as you drizzle in the olive oil until thoroughly emulsified. Stir in the shallots and season with salt and black pepper to taste. Refrigerate until ready to use. The vinaigrette will keep in an airtight container in the fridge for up to 3 days.

Assemble the Salad

On a large serving plate, arrange the endive, arugula, and Asian pear. Drizzle half of the vinaigrette on top, adding more as needed. Sprinkle the crumbled goat cheese and sliced almonds on top right before serving.

Chopped Salad

with Lemony Basil Dressing

¼ cup extra virgin
    olive oil

¼ cup grated
    Parmesan
    cheese, plus
    more for
    sprinkling

¼ cup cashews,
    walnuts, or
    almonds

2 tablespoons
    unseasoned rice
    vinegar

Juice of 1 lemon

1 cup packed fresh
    basil leaves

2 cups packed baby
    spinach, plus
    2 cups chopped

2 tablespoons
    chopped chives

2 cloves garlic,
    minced

1 teaspoon freshly
    ground black
    pepper

½ teaspoon kosher
    salt

6 cups chopped napa
    cabbage

2 Roma tomatoes,
    chopped

1 English cucumber,
    seeds removed,
    chopped

4 ounces pepper
    Jack cheese
    or mozzarella
    cheese, cubed

¼ cup sunflower
    kernels or
    pumpkin seeds

SERVES 2

There are three critical components to making the most fulfilling chopped salad in the whole wide world. First, the ingredients need a variety of textures and flavors. Second, the dressing should pack a punch but not overpower all the other ingredients. Lastly and most importantly, everything MUST be tossed together in a ridiculously large bowl. Is the bowl bigger than your butt? If so, that's the correct one. Not only is it oddly satisfying to freely toss a bunch of stuff in a large bowl, but your salad will also inevitably taste better because every bite will be a perfectly dressed mouthful comprised of a little bit of everything (making those few extra minutes of chopping completely worth it). The bulk of this salad consists of hearty napa cabbage (which is sweeter and more tender than red or green cabbage), juicy tomatoes, crunchy cucumbers, and nutty sunflower kernels. But feel free to add virtually anything else you want, such as a protein, roasted veggies, or even dried fruit—the possibilities are endless. The dressing is packed with a ton of wholesome goodies, like nuts, baby spinach, and garlic, that are blended with fragrant basil and tangy lemon juice, resulting in a full-bodied masterpiece. An added bonus is that both the salad and dressing can be prepared ahead of time. Just be sure to keep them separate until right before serving.

| Make the Dressing | In a blender, first add the oil, Parmesan, cashews, vinegar, and lemon juice. Then add the basil, 2 cups packed spinach, chives, garlic, black pepper, and salt. Blend until smooth. (Adding the liquids first will help the ingredients blend better.) |

| Assemble the Salad | In a very large bowl, combine the cabbage, 2 cups chopped spinach, tomatoes, cucumber, pepper Jack, and sunflower kernels. Add half of the dressing and toss to fully combine, adding more as needed. Divide between two serving bowls, sprinkle with more Parmesan, and serve immediately. |

KALE & CARROT *Salad*
with Miso-Mustard Dressing

People are always asking me how I'm able to stay in shape after consuming as much food as I do. I usually giggle and run away because I hate answering that question. If I said I was one of those people who "just has good genes," I would be lying (and super annoying). I work out more than I'd like to admit, but I have to because I have zero self-control when it comes to food; my stopping point is when I start breathing heavy and my internal organs are begging me to cool the jets. However, there *are* days when I do actually feel empowered to eat on the lighter side, and this is one of the recipes I like to make. The wholesome hearty kale, sweet carrots, and crunchy rice crackers combined with the creamy-tangy miso-mustard dressing are more than enough to satiate my insatiable appetite. If I happen to want extra protein on that particular day, I'll just add a couple of hard-boiled eggs or some shredded chicken and I'm ready to rumble!

¼ cup extra virgin olive oil

¼ cup unsalted cashews, walnuts, or almonds

3 tablespoons unseasoned rice vinegar

2 tablespoons yellow or white miso paste

2 tablespoons coarse-ground Dijon mustard

1 tablespoon honey or maple syrup

½ teaspoon freshly ground black pepper

1 bunch curly, Tuscan, or red kale, thick stems removed and leaves torn into pieces

1 large carrot (any color), peeled and shaved lengthwise with a vegetable peeler

¼ cup crushed rice crackers, for garnish

2 tablespoons chopped cilantro, for garnish

2 scallions, dark green parts only, chopped, for garnish

SERVES 2

Make the Dressing

In a food processor (or blender), combine the oil, cashews, vinegar, miso paste, mustard, honey, black pepper, and 2 tablespoons water and blend until smooth, adding more water as needed to help everything come together.

Assemble the Salad

In a very large bowl, toss together the kale, carrots, and half of the dressing, gently massaging the dressing into the kale leaves and adding more as needed. Divide the dressed greens between two bowls and garnish with the crushed rice crackers, cilantro, and scallions.

HAWAIIAN CHICKEN

Vermicelli Bowl

NUOC CHAM

3 tablespoons fresh
    lime juice

3 tablespoons fish
    sauce

2 tablespoons
    granulated sugar

1 Thai chili, finely
    chopped, or
    ½ teaspoon
    crushed red
    pepper flakes

CHICKEN THIGHS

¼ cup pineapple juice

2 tablespoons ketchup

2 tablespoons
    reduced-sodium
    soy sauce

2 cloves garlic, minced

1 teaspoon grated
    fresh ginger

1½ pounds boneless,
    skinless chicken
    thighs

7 ounces dried rice
    vermicelli noodles

2 cups shredded
    iceberg lettuce

2 medium carrots,
    peeled and cut
    into thin strips

1 cup bean sprouts

½ English cucumber,
    cut into half
    moons

¼ cup fresh cilantro,
    roughly chopped

¼ cup fresh mint,
    roughly chopped

1 cup crunchy wonton
    strips

1 lime, cut into wedges,
    for serving

SERVES 4

You know when your mind is telling you to eat a salad, but your body is begging you for some carbs? That's me every day, but luckily, I'm a genius and have found the perfect solution! This quintessential hybrid recipe is what you would get if a gorgeous salad and some flirty noodles made love and had a baby. The noodles give it body. The crunchy veggies and fragrant herbs give it beauty. And those juicy, thick (chicken) thighs make it sexy as hell. Finish it off with some sweet-and-salty nuoc cham sauce and you have a complete dish that combines a little bit of everything that you need in your life, while keeping you feeling light and emotionally fulfilled.

Make the Nuoc Cham

In a small bowl, whisk together the lime juice, fish sauce, sugar, chili, and ¼ cup of water until the sugar dissolves. Cover with plastic wrap and refrigerate until needed.

Marinate the Chicken

In a small bowl, whisk together the pineapple juice, ketchup, soy sauce, garlic, and ginger until combined. Transfer to a large freezer bag along with the chicken thighs and seal, squeezing out as much air as possible. Gently massage the marinade into the meat and refrigerate for at least 4 hours or up to 2 days.

Cook the Noodles

Position a rack in the center of the broiler and preheat the broiler to high. Line a large rimmed baking sheet with aluminum foil. Arrange the marinated chicken thighs in an even layer on the prepared baking sheet and let them come to room temperature, about 30 minutes. Discard the excess marinade. In the meantime, cook the noodles according to the package directions. Drain and rinse with cold water. Divide the cooked noodles among four serving bowls and set aside until needed.

Cook the Chicken

Broil the chicken until it is cooked through and charred around the edges, 14 to 16 minutes. Let rest for 15 minutes, then slice into strips.

Assemble the Bowl

Divide the lettuce, carrots, bean sprouts, and cucumbers among the bowls with the noodles. Top with the chicken slices, cilantro, mint, and wonton strips. Serve with the nuoc cham sauce and lime wedges on the side.

EASY GOLDEN EGG
Fried Rice

3 cups cooked
   short-grain
   rice (brown
   or white),
   preferably day-
   old

4 large eggs, whites
   and yolks
   separated

Kosher salt

Ground white
   pepper

2 tablespoons extra
   virgin olive oil,
   divided

½ cup chopped
   Chinese sausage
   (or 4 slices
   chopped bacon)

½ small onion, finely
   chopped

1 teaspoon grated
   fresh ginger

2 cloves garlic,
   minced

SERVES 4

Tip

*Frozen cooked rice
will also work for this
recipe. Just make sure
you thaw it completely
in the fridge before
starting.*

My mom has this huge-ass rice cooker that she uses to make an absurd amount of rice at least twice a week . . . and I absolutely love it because, in case you didn't know, I F*CKING LOVE RICE. She inevitably makes so much rice that even I can't finish it, but that's okay because it means only one thing the next day—*fried* rice! Something magical happens when you stir-fry day-old rice with a few eggs, some aromatics, and Chinese sausage (which happens to be on par with bacon in terms of delectability). Chinese sausage, a.k.a. lap cheong, is an intensely flavored, air-cured sausage (usually made from pork) that's uniquely sweet and salty. It can be found in the refrigerated section at the Asian grocery store and lasts for a really long time in the fridge. If you can't find it, don't worry; bacon will also work beautifully in this recipe. And although there are a lot of fried rice recipes out there, I swear my mom's is the best in all the land . . . and lucky for you, I love to share.

Prep the Rice	In a large bowl, mix together the rice, egg yolks, and ¼ teaspoon each of salt and ground white pepper until all the rice grains are completely coated in egg yolk, making sure to break up any clumps of rice.
Cook the Egg Whites	In a large nonstick skillet or wok over medium-low heat, add 1 tablespoon of the oil. When the oil is hot, add the egg whites and season with salt and white pepper. Cook until the whites are almost set but still very wet looking, 30 to 45 seconds, using a silicone spatula to constantly push them around the skillet (scraping the edges and bottom to ensure even cooking). Transfer to a plate and set aside.
Cook the Aromatics	In the same skillet over medium heat, add the remaining tablespoon of oil. Add the Chinese sausage, onion, and a pinch of salt and cook until the sausage is cooked through and the onions begin to brown, 5 to 7 minutes, stirring occasionally. Add the ginger and garlic and cook until fragrant, 30 to 45 seconds, stirring continuously.
Cook the Rice	Add the rice mixture to the skillet and toss to combine, breaking up any large clumps of rice. Spread the rice evenly in the skillet and cook, undisturbed, until it begins to crisp up on the bottom (maybe even get a little brown), 4 to 5 minutes. Add the cooked egg whites to the skillet and cook for 1 more minute, tossing continuously to combine. Divide among four bowls and serve.

Mama Woo's
MINCED BEEF & RICE *Bowls*

There's something so cozy and welcoming about a big bowl of warm rice topped with seasoned ground beef and a soft cooked egg. It's like a hug and kiss from your favorite human being, but even better because it's edible. This dish is instant comfort food, not to mention insanely quick and easy to throw together. My mom made it for my sisters and me when we were growing up (and still does to this day). My older sister makes it for her kids. And I make it for Doug. What I'm ultimately saying here is that once you make this dish, you are now a part of the crazy Woo family whether you like it or not. Enjoy!

Marinate the Beef	In a medium bowl, whisk together the oyster sauce, cornstarch, ginger, sesame oil, soy sauce, black pepper, and garlic until combined. Add the ground beef and use your hands (or chopsticks) to mix everything together until just combined. Do not overmix or the meat will get tough. Marinate for 20 minutes at room temperature (or overnight in the fridge).
Cook the Beef	In a medium skillet over medium heat, add the ground beef mixture, breaking up any large chunks with a wooden spatula. Spread the beef into an even layer and let cook, undisturbed, until the fat is rendered and the beef is browned and caramelized, 6 to 7 minutes. Add the peas and chicken broth and stir to combine. Bring everything to a boil and scrape the bottom of the skillet with the spatula to loosen all those delicious, browned bits.
Add the Eggs	Reduce the heat to a simmer and create 2 evenly spaced wells in the meat mixture. Crack an egg into a small bowl and gently slide it into one of the wells. Repeat with the other egg. Simmer until the egg whites are just set but the yolks are still runny, 5 to 6 minutes. Divide the rice between two serving bowls, top with the beef and eggs, and garnish with scallions.

2 tablespoons oyster sauce

2 teaspoons cornstarch

2 teaspoons grated fresh ginger

2 teaspoons toasted sesame oil

2 teaspoons reduced-sodium soy sauce

½ teaspoon freshly ground black pepper

1 clove garlic, minced

1 pound ground beef (preferably 85% lean)

½ cup frozen green peas, thawed

½ cup chicken broth, homemade (see page 182) or store-bought, or water

2 large eggs

2 cups cooked rice, for serving

2 scallions, dark green parts only, chopped, for garnish

SERVES 2

Hot & Sour Turkey Soup

with Spinach & Egg

2 tablespoons extra virgin olive oil

1 medium onion, finely chopped

½ teaspoon kosher salt

½ teaspoon ground white pepper

1 pound ground turkey

1 cup stemmed and sliced shiitake mushrooms

4 cups chicken broth, homemade (see page 182) or store-bought

2 tablespoons unseasoned rice vinegar

1 tablespoon reduced-sodium soy sauce

1 tablespoon hot sauce (such as Cholula; optional)

1 tablespoon tahini

2 teaspoons grated fresh ginger

4 large eggs, beaten

2 cups packed baby spinach, roughly chopped

Toasted sesame oil, for garnish

Crusty bread (grilled or toasted), for serving

SERVES 4

As a proud Asian American, I am very passionate about not wasting food and always try my damn hardest to use up all my produce before it goes bad. That's why I love this hot and sour soup. Not only is it absolutely scrumdiddlyumptious as is, it's also a "kitchen sink soup," into which you can toss all your about-to-go-bad vegetables and call it a day (just give those veggies a rough chop first). This soup isn't too hot or too sour (although you can always add more hot sauce or rice vinegar if you prefer), and it's a meal all on its own. The swirled-in eggs give this hearty, nutritious, and flavor-packed soup a creamy and luxurious feel, so whichever way you end up making it—following the recipe exactly or customizing it to your own preferences—I know you're going to feel really good when devouring it.

Cook the Onions & Turkey

In a large soup pot over medium heat, add the oil, onions, salt, and white pepper and cook until the onions are translucent and lightly browned, 7 to 9 minutes, stirring occasionally. Add the ground turkey and mushrooms and cook until the turkey is browned, breaking up any large chunks with a wooden spatula, 4 to 5 minutes.

Make the Soup

Stir in the broth, vinegar, soy sauce, hot sauce, tahini, and ginger and bring to a boil. Reduce the heat to a simmer and gently stir in the eggs until the soup is "creamy" with small flecks of egg scattered throughout. Simmer until just heated through, about 5 minutes. Stir in the spinach and remove from the heat. Divide the soup into serving bowls. Drizzle a little toasted sesame oil on top and serve with crusty bread.

Chunky Corn
& SWEET POTATO
Chowder

Everyone can agree that chowders are delicious, but that's because they're 85% heavy cream and 15% potatoes. While I'm not opposed to slurping up a big bowl of hot cream with a side of potatoes, my body would not like me if I guzzled chowder as often as I crave it. Listen, I'm trying my best to keep this jelly together for all you thirsty folks out there. That's why I've created something that scratches that chowder itch without sacrificing the thick, creamy goodness we want and expect. To the beautiful human reading this, I introduce my chunky corn and sweet potato chowder. The secret to making this soup thick and chowder-y while keeping things on the lighter side is blitzing half of it until it's super silky and smooth, then adding it back to the pot. The result is a hearty chowder filled with large chunks of tender sweet potato and fresh crunchy corn. And to answer the question that I know you want to ask: Yes, of course you can add bacon to it.

1 tablespoon unsalted butter

1 medium onion, chopped

2 cloves garlic, minced

2 cups freshly cut sweet corn kernels (about 4 ears of corn), canned or frozen works too

1 teaspoon all-purpose flour

1 medium sweet potato, peeled and cut into ½-inch pieces

3 cups chicken or vegetable broth

½ cup half-and-half or whole milk

Extra virgin olive oil, for drizzling

2 scallions, dark green parts only, finely chopped, for garnish

SERVES 4

Build the Base

In a large pot over medium heat, melt the butter. When the butter has melted, add the onions and cook until the onions are translucent and slightly browned on the edges, 5 to 7 minutes, stirring occasionally. Stir in the garlic and cook until fragrant, 30 to 45 seconds.

Add More Vegetables

Stir in 1¾ cups of the corn and the flour and cook for 30 to 45 seconds, stirring continuously. Add the sweet potato, broth, and half-and-half and bring to a boil.

Simmer, Blend & Serve

Reduce the heat to a simmer and cook, uncovered, until the sweet potatoes are tender, 15 to 20 minutes. Transfer half of the soup (chunks and all) to a blender and puree until smooth, about 1 minute. Return the pureed soup back to the pot and stir to combine. Divide among four bowls and garnish with a drizzle of olive oil, the remaining ¼ cup of corn, and chopped scallions.

Did You Eat Yet?

TURKEY & MUSHROOM *Collard Green* WRAPS

with Crunchy Peanuts

More often than I would like to own up to, I think of stuffing Five Guys into my mouth and calling it a night. (I have to admit that Five Guys is a questionable name for a burger chain.) So, in order to satisfy my craving for something meaty and burger-like when I also want to be healthy, I'll make these turkey and mushroom wraps. I know this isn't a burger, but the warm turkey-mushroom filling ends up being so meaty, satiating, and packed with umami, I promise you won't even notice the healthy collard green wrap that is keeping it all together. To top it off, the crushed peanuts give it that extra crunch and texture you didn't even know you needed.

Make the Sauce	In a small bowl, whisk together the hoisin, peanut butter, sambal oelek, fish sauce, ginger, garlic, and ¼ cup of water until smooth. Set aside.
Cook the Ingredients	In a large skillet over medium heat, add the sesame oil, ground turkey, salt, and black pepper to taste and cook until browned, 3 to 4 minutes, breaking up any large chunks with a wooden spatula. Add the mushrooms and sauce mixture and cook until the mushrooms release some of their liquid and the sauce thickens, 3 to 4 minutes. Transfer to a serving dish.
Assemble the Wraps	To make a wrap, place a piece of collard green in your palm and top with a helping of the turkey mixture. Garnish with crushed peanuts and a pinch of cilantro before rolling up and sticking in your mouth hole.

2 tablespoons hoisin sauce

2 tablespoons unsweetened natural creamy peanut butter, stirred well

1 tablespoon sambal oelek

1 tablespoon fish sauce

1 tablespoon grated fresh ginger

4 cloves garlic, minced

1 tablespoon toasted sesame oil

1 pound ground turkey

Kosher salt

Freshly ground black pepper

2 cups stemmed and diced shiitake mushrooms

3 large collard greens, stems removed and leafy green parts cut in half

¼ cup crushed roasted peanuts, for garnish

¼ cup finely chopped fresh cilantro, for garnish

SERVES 2

- 2 tablespoons extra virgin olive oil
- 1 medium onion, chopped
- 1 serrano or jalapeño pepper (seeds optional), chopped
- ½ teaspoon kosher salt
- ½ teaspoon freshly ground black pepper
- 3 cloves garlic, minced
- 2 cups cherry tomatoes (about 1 pound), halved
- 1 (15.5-ounce) can chickpeas (a.k.a. garbanzo beans), rinsed and drained
- 2 tablespoons curry powder
- 2 tablespoons sambal oelek (optional)
- 1 (13.5-ounce) can full-fat coconut milk
- 2 tablespoons finely chopped fresh cilantro, for garnish
- 2 cups cooked rice (long or short grain), for serving
- 1 lime, cut into wedges, for serving

SERVES 4

Spicy Coconut Curry CHICKPEA & CHERRY TOMATO *Stew*

Not trying to be dramatic or anything, but there are days when I question my entire existence and wonder if I should stop eating meat. I'm a realistic person, though, and I know that will never happen, so I've settled on Meatless Mondays (although it's usually on Sunday in our household). This is one of my favorite dishes to make when the time comes because all I can think about is how much I actually love eating this dish (which also happens to be vegan). The chickpeas are substantial and filling, the tomatoes are naturally sweet and acidic, and the generous amount of sambal oelek throws in a hot kick. It is such a hearty, satisfying, and well-rounded meal that, regardless of whether you're an herbivore, carnivore, or somewhere in between, you are going to be super happy eating this until the very last bite.

Cook the Vegetables

In a large pot over medium heat, add the oil, onion, serrano, salt, and black pepper and cook until the onions are translucent and lightly browned, 7 to 9 minutes, stirring occasionally. Add the garlic and cook until fragrant, 30 to 45 seconds, stirring continuously. Add the cherry tomatoes and chickpeas and cook until the tomatoes begin to break down and soften, 8 to 10 minutes, stirring occasionally. Add the curry powder and sambal oelek and cook until fragrant, about 30 seconds, stirring continuously.

Finish the Dish

Add the coconut milk and bring to a boil. Reduce the heat to a simmer and cook until the mixture thickens slightly, 5 to 10 minutes. Garnish with cilantro and serve with rice and lime wedges.

I Love Noods

Simply
Kick-Ass
GARLIC
NOODLES

Sometimes you just want a giant bowl of delicious carbs magically delivered straight into your mouth, but sadly I don't think they have an app for that type of service yet (and if you know of one, please DM me). The good news is I have a recipe that is so easy it comes pretty close to that—and it's devilishly good. All you have to do is make a quick sauce, boil some spaghetti, combine the two, and out comes these gorgeous, shiny noodles that taste like the best damn mouth party you've ever been invited to in your entire life. The only slightly tedious part (but totally worth it) is having to peel and mince the garlic.

1 tablespoon oyster sauce

1 tablespoon fish sauce

1 tablespoon sesame oil

1 teaspoon packed brown sugar

2 scallions, dark green parts only, finely chopped

4 tablespoons (½ stick) unsalted butter

8 cloves garlic, minced

12 ounces dried spaghetti or fresh ramen noodles

Freshly grated Parmesan cheese, for garnish

SERVES 4

Tip

If you can find frozen cubes of minced garlic at the grocery store, buy every single package available. Hoarding means nothing to me here, especially when it comes to having to do even less work!

Make the Sauce

Bring a large pot of salted water to a rolling boil. Meanwhile, in a small bowl, whisk together the oyster sauce, fish sauce, sesame oil, brown sugar, and scallions until the sugar dissolves. Set aside. In a large skillet or wok over medium heat, melt the butter. When the butter has melted, add the garlic, and cook until fragrant, 30 to 45 seconds, stirring continuously. Reduce the heat to medium-low and add the sauce mixture. Cook until the scallions have softened, about 45 seconds, stirring often. Turn the heat off.

Cook the Noodles

When the water is boiling, add the spaghetti and cook 1 minute less than al dente according to the package directions. Using tongs, transfer the spaghetti directly into the skillet along with ½ cup of the pasta water. Increase the heat to medium-high and toss the noodles until most of the liquid has been absorbed, 45 to 60 seconds. Divide among four pasta bowls and garnish with a generous amount of Parmesan.

CHILLED

Sesame-Honey Ramen with Chicken & Cucumbers

1 large skin-on, bone-in chicken breast (about ¾ pound)

3 tablespoons extra virgin olive oil, divided

Kosher salt

Freshly ground black pepper

½ cup tahini

2 tablespoons honey

1 tablespoon mayonnaise

1 tablespoon reduced-sodium soy sauce

1 tablespoon yellow or white miso paste

1 teaspoon grated fresh ginger

¼ teaspoon crushed red pepper flakes

1 clove garlic, minced

10 ounces fresh ramen noodles (instant ramen noodles will work in a pinch)

3 to 4 Persian cucumbers or ½ English cucumber, cut into matchsticks

Toasted sesame seeds, for garnish

SERVES 2

Having been with Doug for almost fifteen years, I've discovered the secret to a healthy long-term relationship is being able to agree on what to eat for dinner in a reasonable amount of time. Otherwise, both of you will just get hangry and start fighting about the most ridiculous things in the world. You might say something like, "I'm really pissed off at you for cheating on me in my dream last night" or "Never EVER touch that motherf*cking thermostat again or, swear to God, I will walk out that door." You know, sh*t that could simply be avoided if you just had a go-to dish you both love no matter what kind of indecisive moods you may be in. *This* is that go-to dish for us! The combination of chilled ramen noodles, shredded chicken, and crunchy matchstick cucumbers all mixed together with a smooth, creamy sesame sauce is always the right answer when it comes to saving a relationship—*or* when you just want a delicious and satisfying meal that will put a smile on your belly's face (if it had a face). Anyway, you're welcome for the undeniably awesome recipe and relationship advice.

Roast the Chicken Breast

Position a rack in the center of the oven and preheat the oven to 375ºF. Line a small baking sheet with parchment paper and place the chicken breast in the center. Drizzle with 1 tablespoon of the olive oil and season with salt and black pepper. Roast until the thickest part of the breast reaches 165ºF, 25 to 35 minutes, depending on the size of the breast. Let the chicken rest, uncovered, at room temperature for 15 to 20 minutes. While the chicken is resting, make the sesame sauce and cook the noodles.

Make the Sesame Sauce

Bring a large pot of water to a rolling boil. Meanwhile, in a medium bowl, whisk together the tahini, honey, the remaining 2 tablespoons of olive oil, mayonnaise, soy sauce, miso paste, ginger, pepper flakes, garlic, and ½ cup of water until smooth. Set aside.

Cook the Ramen

Prepare an ice bath by filling a large bowl with cold water and lots of ice. When the pot of water is boiling, add the ramen noodles and cook according to the package directions. Drain and immediately transfer them to the ice bath. Using your hands, gently separate and massage the noodle strands in the ice bath until the noodles are thoroughly chilled, 1 to 2 minutes. ("Massaging" the noodles will give them a chewier texture and prevent them from clumping.) Thoroughly drain the noodles.

Assemble the Dish

Shred the chicken into bite-size pieces, discarding the skin and bones. Transfer to a large bowl along with the ramen noodles, cucumbers, and half of the sesame sauce. Toss until combined, adding more sauce as needed. Garnish with toasted sesame seeds and serve.

DAN DAN–INSPIRED
Zoodles

3 tablespoons extra
  virgin olive oil

2 tablespoons
  sambal oelek

2 tablespoons
  sriracha

2 tablespoons tahini

2 tablespoons
  unsalted butter

½ pound ground
  chicken

½ pound ground pork
  or beef

Kosher salt

Freshly ground black
  pepper

3 scallions, light
  and dark green
  parts only, finely
  chopped

1 Fresno chili or
  jalapeño pepper,
  seeded and
  finely chopped

4 cloves garlic,
  minced

1 pound fresh
  "zoodles" (a.k.a.
  zucchini spirals),
  store-bought or
  homemade

SERVES 4

Before you make a frowny face at the word ZOODLES (a mash-up of the words *zucchini* and *noodles*), just know that I was the biggest skeptic of them all when it came to these noodle impostors. I mean, how could a humble little squash compete with my best frenemy, the carb? Anyway, one week I ate way too many of my frenemies (didn't know that was even possible), so I consciously made the decision to give zoodles a try. Turns out I wasn't mad about it! Do zoodles taste like pasta noodles? No. But are zoodles fun and delicious in an entirely different way? Yes! And they happen to be the perfect vehicle for this satisfyingly spicy, savory sauce. Dan dan sauce originates from Sichuan cuisine and is usually paired with thin noodles, while the word *dan dan* comes from the across-the-shoulder carrying pole that street vendors used to balance the two baskets of noodles and sauce. You're more than welcome to use actual noodles, but personally I think the heat in this meaty sauce pairs beautifully with the twirlable al dente strands of zucchini, resulting in a dish that's both light and satiating at the same time.

| Make the Sauce | In a small bowl, whisk together the oil, sambal oelek, sriracha, and tahini until smooth. Set aside. |

| Cook the Meats | In a large nonstick skillet over medium heat, melt the butter. When the butter has melted, add the ground meats and season with salt and black pepper. Cook until the meat is browned and caramelized, 8 to 10 minutes, using a vegetable masher to break it up into pieces as small as possible, which will help the meaty sauce stick to the zoodles. |

| Add the Aromatics | Add the scallions and chili and cook until tender, 2 to 3 minutes. Add the garlic and cook until fragrant, 30 to 45 seconds, stirring continuously. |

| Finish the Dish | Stir in the prepared sauce and the zoodles. Cook until the zoodles are al dente and the sauce has thickened slightly, 1 to 2 minutes, gently tossing to combine while scraping the bottom of the skillet to loosen any remaining browned bits. (Do not overcook the zoodles or they will get mushy and fall apart.) Divide among four bowls and serve. |

GARLICKY FISH
SAUCE-SPIKED

Tomato Sauce
with Bucatini & Ricotta

- ¼ cup extra virgin olive oil
- 6 cloves garlic, minced
- 10 Roma tomatoes (about 2 pounds), quartered
- 2 tablespoons fish sauce
- 1 tablespoon unsalted butter
- 1 teaspoon freshly ground black pepper
- 12 ounces dried bucatini or spaghetti
- 1 cup whole-milk ricotta cheese
- Grated Parmesan cheese, for serving
- Fresh basil leaves, roughly torn by hand, for garnish

SERVES 4

Make Ahead

The sauce can be made up to 2 days in advance and stored in an airtight container in the fridge (or it can be frozen for up to 3 months). Simply heat up the sauce in a skillet and toss it with cooked pasta and some pasta water for a quick meal any day of the week.

This recipe really feels like home to me. Just to be clear, I'm not talking about my home but the home of some Asian Italian mother I've never actually met. Mama Woo is a brilliant cook—just not when it comes to pasta and tomato sauce. She tends to boil the sh*t out of spaghetti noodles until they're mushy (NO!), then fully drains them (OMG!), before letting them sit in a colander to further soften and dry out (WTF!). Then she tops the noodles with store-bought marinara sauce that, simply put, tastes pretty wonky. For the record, I'll eat my mom's wonky spaghetti any day of the week because she's my mother and she made it, but I promise you this recipe is NOTHING like hers. For starters, I use bucatini, which is like a thick spaghetti with a hole in it that helps to sop up all that saucy goodness (plus, it's just really fun to eat). Next, my quick homemade tomato sauce is fresh and naturally sweet, while the fish sauce provides the perfect amount of umami funk. Lastly, the dollop of ricotta adds just a touch of creaminess that brings it all home. Speaking of home, my imaginary Asian Italian mom would be so proud of me for finding a way to make an Italian-inspired dish also *slightly* Asian.

Make the Sauce

In a large Dutch oven over medium heat, add the olive oil. When the olive oil is hot, add the garlic and cook until fragrant, 30 to 45 seconds, stirring continuously. Stir in the tomatoes, fish sauce, butter, and black pepper. Cover and cook until the tomatoes begin to break down and the skins fall off, 12 to 14 minutes, stirring occasionally. Reduce the heat to a simmer and continue cooking, uncovered, until the tomatoes break down completely and the sauce thickens slightly (but still looks a little runny), 16 to 18 minutes, stirring occasionally and scraping the bottom of the pot with a wooden spatula. When the sauce is done, reduce the heat to the lowest setting and begin cooking the noodles.

Boil the Bucatini

Bring a large pot of salted water to a rolling boil. Add the bucatini and cook 1 minute less than al dente according to the package directions. Using tongs, transfer the noodles directly into the sauce along with ¼ cup of pasta water. Cook over medium heat until the sauce thickens and coats the noodles, 1 to 2 minutes, tossing continuously and adding a little more pasta water as needed to reach the desired consistency.

Finish the Dish

Divide among four pasta bowls, then top with the ricotta and a generous amount of grated Parmesan. Garnish with the torn basil leaves and serve immediately.

RED CURRY
Mac 'n' Cheese

8 ounces elbow macaroni

4 tablespoons (½ stick) unsalted butter

2 cloves garlic, minced

¼ cup all-purpose flour

2 tablespoons tomato paste

2 tablespoons Thai red curry paste

2 (12-ounce) cans evaporated milk

1 cup half-and-half

4 ounces Monterey or Gruyère cheese, freshly shredded

4 ounces sharp Cheddar cheese, freshly shredded

TOPPING

¼ cup crushed butter crackers

1 tablespoon unsalted butter, melted

¼ teaspoon freshly ground black pepper

SERVES 4

I promise you I am not a mac 'n' cheese snob. In fact, I have seven boxes of Kraft's famous original taking up valuable real estate in my pantry at this exact moment. I will literally devour any type of mac 'n' cheese—whether homemade or not—placed within a ten-foot radius of my mouth. That said, there is something uniquely cozy and comforting about homemade mac 'n' cheese that no mass-produced version can rival. My recipe calls for a little bit of Thai red curry paste and tomato paste in the cheese sauce, resulting in a dish that is bold and fun but also familiar. I like to transfer everything to a baking dish and top it off with crushed butter crackers for some crunchy goodness just before sliding the entire thing into the oven to brown up. If you aren't a fan of curry paste or even tomato paste, simply omit one (or both) from the recipe and you'll end up with a more traditional version. Alternatively, you can increase the amount of curry paste if that's a flavor you really love. You can't go wrong either way; just remember to use freshly shredded cheese (off the block), which will create a smoother sauce than if you use the preshredded variety.

Boil the Macaroni

Position a rack in the top of the oven and preheat the oven to 400°F. Bring a large pot of salted water to a rolling boil. Add the macaroni and cook for 2 minutes less than al dente according to the package directions. Drain (do not rinse) and set aside.

Make the Sauce

In a large pot over medium-high heat, melt the butter. When the butter has melted, add the garlic and cook until just fragrant, 30 to 45 seconds, whisking continuously. Sprinkle in the flour and cook until just barely golden brown, about 1 minute, whisking continuously. Add the tomato paste and curry paste and whisk until fully combined. Whisk in the evaporated milk and half-and-half and bring to a boil. Reduce the heat to a simmer and cook until the mixture is thick enough to coat the back of a spoon, about 5 minutes, whisking occasionally. Turn the heat off, add the shredded cheeses, and whisk until melted. Add the cooked macaroni and stir until fully combined. Transfer the macaroni mixture to a 1.5-quart baking dish. It will seem like there is way too much cheese sauce, but most of it will get absorbed by the pasta once it's baked.

Make the Topping

In a small bowl, combine the crushed butter crackers, melted butter, and black pepper. Toss until fully combined and sprinkle the mixture all over the macaroni. Bake until golden brown on top, 8 to 10 minutes. Serve warm.

Shanghai Rice Cakes

12 ounces rice cakes (oval slices or long cylinders)

¼ cup chicken stock or water

2 tablespoons oyster sauce

1 tablespoon reduced-sodium soy sauce

1 teaspoon packed brown sugar (light or dark)

1 teaspoon unseasoned rice vinegar

2 cloves garlic, minced

1 tablespoon canola oil

½ pound large shrimp, peeled and deveined

2 cups stemmed and sliced shiitake mushrooms

2 scallions, light and dark green parts only, chopped

2 cups chopped napa cabbage or green cabbage

2 cups packed baby spinach, roughly chopped

SERVES 4

There are some people who are perfectly happy eating the same thing every day—I'm just not one of them. I wish I were because staying in shape would be so much easier! I've tried weekly meal prepping, but by the third day of eating the same thing, my body refuses to register what I'm eating as actual food. However, I will say that if I did have to eat one thing for the rest of my life, it would be these stir-fried rice cakes or, as we say in Cantonese, "chao nian gao." Chewy rice cakes, succulent shrimp, and crunchy cabbage are quickly tossed together in a slightly sweet-and-savory sauce. Whether my mom made it or we ordered it at a restaurant, chao nian gao has been my favorite thing to eat ever since I was a teeny-tiny little tater tot and, not surprisingly, it still is to this day. Rice cakes can be found at your local Asian supermarket and come in a variety of shapes and sizes, so I highly recommend you seek them out and give them a try. If unopened, they last for a long-ass time in your fridge (and even longer in the freezer). Trust me on this one; you'll thank me later.

Prep the Rice Cakes	Prepare the rice cakes for cooking according to the package directions and set aside.
Make the Sauce	In a small bowl, whisk together the stock, oyster sauce, soy sauce, brown sugar, vinegar, and garlic until the sugar dissolves. Set aside.
Cook the Shrimp	In a large skillet or wok over medium heat, add the oil. When the oil is hot, add the shrimp and cook until opaque and curled up, about 1 minute on each side. Transfer to a plate and set aside.
Cook the Vegetables	To the same skillet over medium heat, add the mushrooms and scallions and cook until the mushrooms are browned and slightly shrunken, 3 to 4 minutes, tossing occasionally. Add the prepared sauce and rice cakes and cook until the rice cakes are warm, 2 to 3 minutes, separating any that are stuck together (they will still be slightly firm at this point). Add the cabbage and spinach and cook until the rice cakes have softened and the spinach has wilted, 1 to 2 minutes, tossing continuously. Remove from the heat.
Finish the Dish	Add the cooked shrimp to the skillet and gently toss to combine. Transfer to a serving plate and serve immediately.

PAPPARDELLE
with Lamb, Shiitakes & Egg Yolk

2 tablespoons extra
    virgin olive oil,
    plus more for
    drizzling

½ pound ground lamb

Kosher salt

Freshly ground black
    pepper

2 cups stemmed and
    sliced shiitake
    mushrooms

3 scallions, light
    and dark green
    parts only,
    chopped

3 cloves garlic,
    minced

8 ounces pappardelle
    egg noodles
    (dried or fresh)

1 cup freshly grated
    Parmesan
    or Pecorino
    Romano cheese,
    plus more for
    garnish

2 large egg yolks, for
    garnish

SERVES 2

Ever since I started The Delicious Cook, I've learned that there's nothing better than being your own boss—except maybe marrying rich. Then you wouldn't have to work at all. Oh well, too late for me now! Besides, who needs a private island or a pasta maker anyway? Also, when I say pasta maker, I mean an actual human who makes fresh pasta. I guess I'll just have to settle for pappardelle and a husband who loves me for me. I'm just kidding—eating pappardelle is not settling! Pappardelle noodles feel fancy, and the dried version actually comes pretty close to tasting like freshly made noodles. Another great thing is that pappardelle pairs well with full-flavored ingredients, like the rich, caramelized lamb and umami-tastic shiitakes that are found in this recipe. This dish is meaty, eggy, and bougie all at once! And as much as I love pregrated Parmesan, I find that freshly grated works best here in order to get a smooth, silky sauce. After making this, you'll feel like a million bucks without really having done much work . . . kind of like marrying rich.

Cook the Lamb	In a large skillet over medium heat, add the olive oil and ground lamb and season with salt and black pepper. Cook until the lamb is browned and caramelized, 6 to 7 minutes, breaking up any large chunks with a wooden spatula.
Cook the Mushrooms	Bring a large pot of salted water to a rolling boil. Meanwhile, add the mushrooms, scallions, and garlic to the skillet and cook until the mushrooms are browned and slightly shrunken, 3 to 4 minutes, stirring occasionally. Reduce the heat to the lowest setting.
Cook the Pappardelle	When the water is boiling, add the pappardelle and cook for 2 minutes less than al dente according to the package directions. Using tongs, transfer the noodles directly to the skillet along with 1 cup of pasta water and the Parmesan. Increase the heat to medium and toss continuously until the sauce has thickened, 2 to 3 minutes, adding more pasta water as needed. Divide between two pasta bowls and drizzle with a generous amount of olive oil. Garnish each bowl with an egg yolk and more freshly grated Parmesan. Mix the egg yolk into the noodles while the dish is still hot before shoveling the noodles straight into your face.

Spicy ALMOND PESTO *Udon*

with Baby Spinach & Burrata

½ cup Garlicky Almond & Spinach Pesto (page 28)

1 tablespoon fish sauce

2 teaspoons crushed red pepper flakes

14 ounces fresh udon noodles

2 cups packed baby spinach

4 ounces burrata cheese

SERVES 2

In the noodle world, ramen and spaghetti are always in the limelight, but what about the gorgeous and voluptuous udon noodle? I'm an equal opportunity noodle lover, and I think udon deserves a little more lovin' than it usually gets. Like I always say, if you have a girthy noodle, you're bound to have a good time (that's why I don't like angel hair . . . but that's okay, no one likes angel hair). Most people think udon belongs only in a broth, but these springy, toothsome noods are just begging to be used in other ways. Which brings me to this recipe—thick, sexy strands of chewy udon are tossed with my warm spicy almond pesto and some baby spinach, then served topped with luscious burrata cheese for a decadent, creamy finish. This simple but exciting combination is not only unexpected, it's the mash-up you had no idea you were craving . . . until now.

Tip

Make sure you get fresh udon noodles (in the refrigerated section) and NOT the dried kind (which are notoriously mediocre). If you can't find fresh udon, just about any other type of noodle will work for this recipe (except angel hair).

Make the Sauce

Bring a large pot of unsalted water to a rolling boil. Meanwhile, in a large skillet over medium heat, add the pesto, fish sauce, and pepper flakes and cook until the sauce is warm, 2 to 3 minutes, stirring continuously. Reduce the heat to the lowest possible setting while you cook the udon.

Cook the Udon

When the water is boiling, add the udon and cook until al dente according to the package directions (do not overcook!). Using tongs or a spider, transfer the udon directly to the sauce in the skillet. Add the spinach and gently toss everything together until the spinach is just wilted, about 1 minute. Divide between two pasta bowls and top with the burrata before serving.

WHITE WINE–BRAISED *Pork Ragù* with LOOSE LASAGNA NOODLES →

My husband is one of the most ah-mazing human beings that has ever walked the face of this planet and one of the few people who don't annoy me (which is good since we're married). However, as perfect as he is, the man still has his flaws—and one of them is how he eats noodles. Brace yourself: he will take a whole mouthful of noodles, bite through them, and let the rest fall back into the bowl! A little bit of me dies every time he does this, but I just tell myself over and over again that he loves me for me until the horror wears off. Luckily for him (and me), this pasta dish *actually* requires a knife and fork. Juicy, fatty pork shoulder is braised with white wine and garlic, resulting in an intensely flavored braise-sauce hybrid. Once the pork is fall-apart tender, all that gorgeousness gets tossed with hefty lasagna noodles and you get one of the most comforting and substantial dishes you will ever encounter in your life. This time (and only this time), noodle biting is actually encouraged.

1 pound pork shoulder or butt, cut into four equal pieces

2 tablespoons canola oil, divided

Kosher salt

Freshly ground black pepper

½ medium onion, finely chopped

4 cloves garlic, minced

1 tablespoon sambal oelek (optional)

1 cup dry white wine

3 cups chicken broth, homemade (see page 182) or store-bought

¼ cup heavy cream

12 ounces dry wavy lasagna noodles

Shaved Pecorino Romano cheese, for serving

SERVES 4

Sear the Pork

Position a rack in the center of the oven and preheat the oven to 375°F. Use a paper towel to pat dry the pork. Drizzle 1 tablespoon of the oil all over the pork and generously season all sides with salt and black pepper. In a large Dutch oven over medium heat, add the pork pieces and cook, undisturbed, until golden brown and caramelized, 4 to 5 minutes on each side, adjusting the heat as needed so the meat doesn't burn. Transfer the seared pork to a plate.

Cook the Aromatics

To the same Dutch oven over medium heat, add the remaining oil and onions and cook until translucent and lightly charred on the edges, 7 to 9 minutes, stirring occasionally. Add the garlic and sambal oelek (if using) and cook until fragrant, 30 to 45 seconds, stirring continuously. Add the wine and cook for 1 minute, loosening any browned bits on the bottom of the pot with a wooden spatula. Add the broth and cooked pork and bring to a boil.

Braise the Pork

Turn the heat off and cover the Dutch oven with the lid. Transfer to the oven and braise until the pork is fall-apart tender, 1½ to 2 hours, depending on the thickness of the pork pieces. If desired, skim off any rendered fat from the surface of the sauce (I personally love the extra flavor). Use two large forks to shred the pork, then stir in the heavy cream. Keep warm on the stovetop on the lowest heat setting while you cook the noodles.

Cook the Noodles

Bring a large pot of salted water to a rolling boil. Add the lasagna noodles and boil for 3 minutes less than al dente according to the package directions. Using tongs, transfer the noodles and ½ cup of pasta water directly into the Dutch oven and gently toss together (it's okay if a noodle or two break). Don't dump the pasta water just in case you need to loosen the sauce a bit more. Cover the Dutch oven with the lid and cook over medium-low heat until the noodles are al dente and the sauce has thickened slightly, 3 to 4 minutes, adding more pasta water if needed to loosen up the sauce. Keep in mind the sauce will be pretty thin at first but will start to thicken up as the noodles absorb the liquid and finish cooking. Divide among four pasta bowls and garnish with a generous amount of shaved Pecorino Romano before serving.

MAMA WOO'S

Pork & Shrimp **Wontons** ➜

½ pound ground pork

½ pound shrimp, peeled and deveined, finely chopped

2 tablespoons minced chives (fresh or dried)

1 tablespoon reduced-sodium soy sauce

1 tablespoon toasted sesame oil, plus more for drizzling

1 teaspoon packed brown sugar (light or dark)

½ teaspoon kosher salt

½ teaspoon freshly ground black pepper

36 wonton wrappers, store-bought

6 cups chicken broth, homemade (see page 182) or store-bought

Fresh cilantro, for garnish

Serrano peppers, thinly sliced, for garnish

MAKES 36 WONTONS

Tip

To prevent the stack of wonton wrappers from drying out while you wrap the wontons, cover them with a damp paper towel.

When I was a little doe-eyed youngster, I would sit at the kitchen counter and watch my mom expertly wrap what seemed like a bajillion wontons. As I patiently observed her make one of my favorite comfort foods in the entire world, she would make it very clear that she made wontons *only* for the people she loved . . . right before asking me how many of them I wanted for dinner. Now that I'm a grown-ass man, I also make wontons for the people I love and, luckily, my mom's recipe is so easy it's not that hard to show a lot of people some love. Since the foolproof filling is a quick mix of ground pork, shrimp, and some pantry staples, the "toughest" part is wrapping them. But don't worry, after the first few you'll quickly get the hang of it and become a wonton wrapping machine! These fast-cooking dumplings are perfect on their own but also happen to pair wonderfully with my Smoky Chili Coconut Oil (page 26) or Everything Sauce (page 29).

| Make the Filling | In a large bowl, mix together the ground pork, shrimp, chives, soy sauce, sesame oil, brown sugar, salt, and black pepper until just combined. Do not overmix. |

| Wrap the Wontons | Line a baking sheet with parchment paper. Place a wonton wrapper in the palm of your hand and, using your finger, moisten the border with a little water. Spoon about 2 teaspoons of filling into the center of the wrapper and carefully bring the opposite corners together, pinching along the seams to seal, or follow the step-by-step images on the next page to wrap the wontons. Place the finished wonton on the prepared baking sheet and repeat with the remaining filling and wrappers. |

| Cook the Wontons | In a medium pot, bring the broth to a simmer. While the broth is heating up, bring a large pot of unsalted water to a rolling boil. Carefully drop the wontons one at a time into the boiling water, making sure not to overcrowd the pot. Boil just until they float to the surface, 3 to 4 minutes, stirring occasionally so they don't stick to the bottom of the pot. Divide the cooked wontons into bowls and top with a couple of ladles of the broth. Add a drizzle of sesame oil and garnish with cilantro and serrano slices right before serving. |

| Storage | Although uncooked wontons will get mushy if stored in the fridge, the good news is that they freeze beautifully! Place them on a parchment paper–lined plate in the freezer for a couple of hours. Once firm, transfer them to a freezer bag and store in the freezer for up to 6 months. When you want to eat them, cook them exactly how you would fresh wontons, adding a few minutes to the boiling time. |

Swallowtail Fold	Fortune Teller Fold	Bonnet Fold
step 1	step 1	step 1
step 2	step 2	step 2
step 3	step 3	step 3
Finished Wonton	Finished Wonton	Finished Wonton

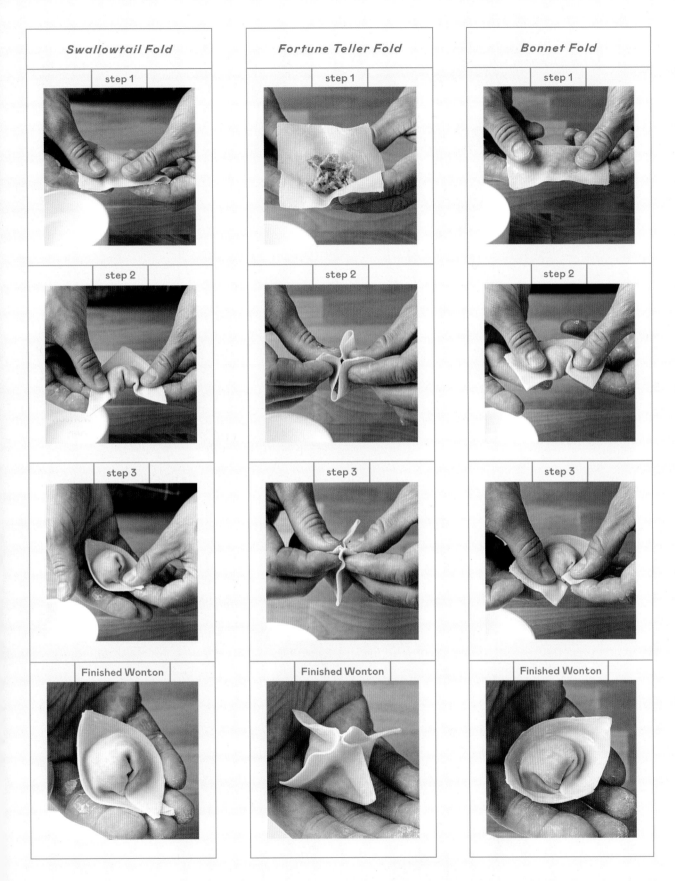

Hot Chili *Hand-Pulled* NOODLES

HAND-PULLED NOODLES

2 cups all-purpose flour

½ teaspoon baking soda

½ teaspoon kosher salt

¾ cup plus 1 tablespoon warm water

Canola oil, for coating

HOT CHILI SAUCE

2 tablespoons unsalted butter

½ pound ground chicken, pork, or lamb

2 teaspoons grated fresh ginger

2 cloves garlic, minced

2 tablespoons reduced-sodium soy sauce

1 tablespoon sambal oelek

1 tablespoon chili powder

1 teaspoon packed brown sugar (light or dark)

SERVES 2

There is nothing sexier than someone who knows how to use their hands . . . to make noodles. Sure, I will happily inhale a huge bowl of store-bought pasta any day of the week, but hand-pulled noodles are on an entirely different level. They are irresistibly chewy, springy, and surprisingly simple to make (plus they don't need to be perfect). Just a little bit of elbow grease will reward you with a big payoff. Hand-pulled noodles are absolutely scrumptious in a soup but equally as yummy when cooked with a sauce, thanks to all the sauce-catching imperfections of each noodle. Similar to what I want in a lover, the hot chili sauce in this recipe is meaty, just spicy enough, and satisfies my needs. Although this is not a straightforward pasta dish, the magical trifecta of ground meat, butter, and sambal oelek results in something that's unexpected and satiating. Once you have the noodles pulled, this recipe comes together in no time, so you'll be moaning and groaning faster than you can say *kumquat* (that's your safe word, too, right?). If you are short on time, feel free to use store-bought pasta (such as fettucine or pappardelle), but just in case I wasn't clear earlier, hand-pulled noodles are next level.

Make the Dough

In the bowl of a stand mixer fitted with the dough hook attachment, combine the flour, baking soda, and salt. Slowly add the warm water to the center of the mixture and mix on medium-low speed until shaggy, 1 to 2 minutes. If the dough looks dry, add water, a teaspoon at a time, until all the flour is hydrated. Scrape down the sides of the bowl and continue mixing on medium speed until a firm dough forms (it won't be super smooth), 2 to 3 minutes. (Alternatively, if you don't have a stand mixer, mix the ingredients together in a large bowl until shaggy, then scrape the dough out onto a clean surface and knead until firm.) Wrap the dough in plastic wrap and let it rest at room temperature for about 2 hours or refrigerate for up to 2 days (the dough may darken in color but is totally safe to eat). Let it come to room temperature before making the noodles.

<table>
<tr><td>

Make the
Noodles

</td><td>

Bring a large pot of salted water to a rolling boil. Meanwhile, divide the ball of dough in half and, using a rolling pin, flatten each into a ¼-inch-thick oval. Lightly coat both sides of each oval with a thin layer of oil. Using a pastry wheel or pizza cutter, cut the oval widthwise into ½-inch-thick strips. Working with one strip at a time, gently stretch to approximately one forearm's length, occasionally "smacking" the noodle on the table to help stretch it before wrapping it around your hand. Set the pulled noodle aside and continue with the remaining strips of dough.

</td></tr>
<tr><td>

Cook the
Noodles

</td><td>

Carefully drop the noodles into the boiling water and cook until just al dente, 45 to 60 seconds. (If your pot is on the smaller side, cook the noodles in batches so they don't get mushy and stick together.) Once cooked, transfer the noodles to a colander, rinse with cool water, and set aside until needed.

</td></tr>
<tr><td>

Brown the
Meat

</td><td>

In a large skillet over medium heat, melt the butter. When the butter has melted, add the ground chicken, and cook until browned and caramelized, 7 to 9 minutes, breaking up any large chunks with a wooden spatula.

</td></tr>
<tr><td>

Make the
Sauce

</td><td>

Add the ginger and garlic to the skillet. Cook until fragrant, about 30 seconds, stirring continuously. Add the soy sauce, sambal oelek, chili powder, and brown sugar. Cook until the sugar dissolves, about 30 seconds, scraping the bottom of the skillet with the wooden spatula to loosen any browned bits.

</td></tr>
<tr><td>

Add the
Noodles

</td><td>

Add the cooked noodles to the sauce and cook on medium-high heat until the noodles are coated and everything is hot, 1 to 2 minutes, tossing the noodles continuously. Divide between two bowls and serve immediately.

</td></tr>
</table>

Make Ahead

Always cook hand-pulled noodles as soon as possible, since the texture of raw noodles will change if not cooked soon after pulling. To store, place unsauced boiled noodles in an airtight container or freezer bag in the fridge for up to 2 days or in the freezer for up to 3 months. To prepare the noodles for a recipe, blanch the frozen noodles in boiling water until just warm, about 30 seconds. Drain and use as desired.

How to Make Hand-Pulled Noodles

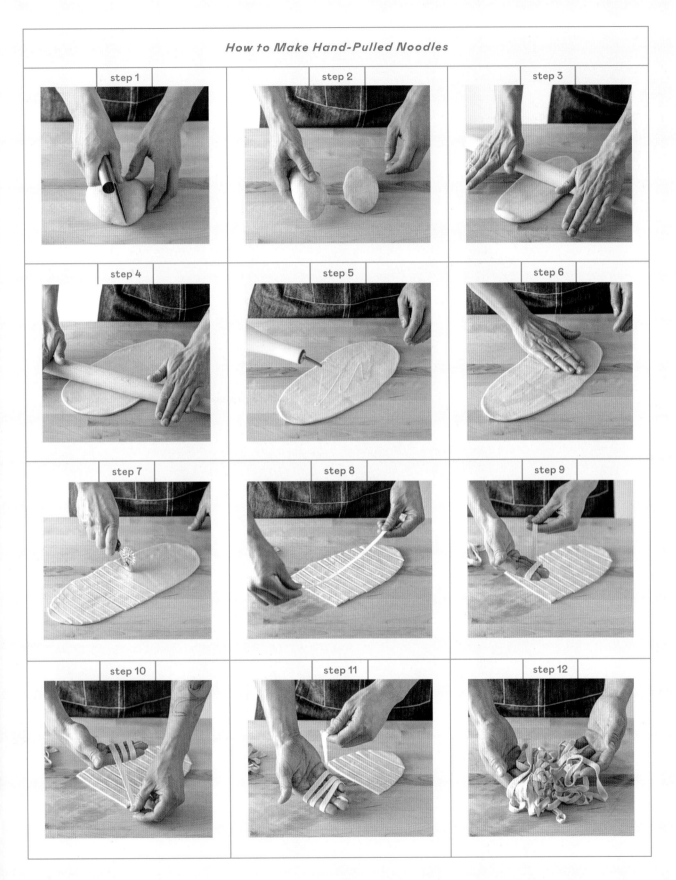

step 1

step 2

step 3

step 4

step 5

step 6

step 7

step 8

step 9

step 10

step 11

step 12

SPICY MISO
Ramen Soup
with Collard Greens

Devouring a huge bowl of hot ramen soup is quite possibly one of the most satisfying things you could do after a long, exhausting day. As soon as I start eating ramen, the steam from the broth makes my entire face sweat, my eyes cross, and my difficult-to-style Asian hair puff out like I'm in a tropical rainforest. But all I can think about is how happy I am eating these savory, chewy strands of perfection. Traditional ramen broth can take up to two full days to make, but I just don't have the patience for that—I need my ramen fix and I need it now! That's why this recipe is everything because it delivers a 20-minute, full-bodied broth that also just happens to be vegan. The miso paste gives it immense flavor, the tahini makes it luscious, and the aromatics balance everything out. I always have fresh ramen noodles in my fridge (or freezer), but since this is a nonjudgmental cookbook, you should feel absolutely no shame in subbing them with the instant variety (just skip the seasoning packet)!

1 tablespoon toasted sesame oil

3-inch piece fresh ginger, sliced

½ large yellow onion, thinly sliced

2 cloves garlic, minced

½ cup yellow miso paste (if using red miso paste, reduce to ¼ cup)

¼ cup tahini

2 tablespoons sambal oelek, plus more for serving (optional)

1 cup unsweetened cashew milk

14 ounces fresh ramen noodles

6 large collard greens, stems removed and leafy green parts thinly sliced

4 sheets nori or seaweed snacks

2 soft-boiled eggs or Jammy Ramen Eggs (page 127), halved

SERVES 2

| Make the Broth | In a large pot over medium-high heat, add the sesame oil, ginger, and onions and cook until the onions soften and slightly char on the edges, 6 to 8 minutes, stirring often. Add the garlic and cook until fragrant, about 30 seconds, stirring continuously. Add the miso paste, tahini, and sambal oelek (if using) and whisk until combined. Add the cashew milk and whisk until the mixture dissolves completely. Whisk in 4 cups of water and bring to a boil. Reduce the heat to a simmer while you cook the noodles. |

| Cook the Ramen | Bring a large pot of unsalted water to a rolling boil. Add the ramen noodles and cook according to the package directions. Transfer the cooked noodles directly into two soup bowls. Add the collard greens to the simmering miso broth and cook until just wilted, 45 to 60 seconds. Divide the wilted greens and broth between the bowls. Top with the nori, additional sambal oelek (if using), and a soft-boiled egg and serve immediately. |

Did Someone Say Snacks?

Warm Spicy WHITE BEAN DIP

People will happily gobble up gallons of hummus, but when you say the words "bean dip" everyone goes dead inside. I guess it doesn't help that some genius thought writing a song that goes, "Beans, beans, the magical fruit, the more you eat, the more you toot!" would further the cause. Personally, I think bean dips are one of the snackiest snacks you could ever have: easy to prepare, healthy, and remarkably versatile in terms of texture, flavor, and even temperature. You are more than welcome to start with dried beans for this recipe, but I don't see why you would since the canned ones are nearly as cheap, nutritionally equivalent, and much less work to prepare. This recipe calls for a blend of cannellini (for texture) and navy beans (for creaminess), which are spruced up by fresh lemon juice and tangy sour cream. I like to serve this smooth, creamy concoction while it's still warm with a side of crunchy potato chips for dunking. Regardless of how you serve it, just make sure you get situated on the couch because you're about to have your mind blown by a bean dip.

1 (15.5-ounce) can cannellini beans, rinsed and drained

1 (15.5-ounce) can navy beans, rinsed and drained

¼ cup sour cream or plain Greek yogurt

2 tablespoons fresh lemon juice

1 tablespoon toasted sesame oil, plus more for garnish

1 tablespoon sriracha, plus more for garnish

1 clove garlic, minced

½ teaspoon kosher salt

½ teaspoon freshly ground black pepper, plus more for garnish

Extra virgin olive oil, for garnish

2 tablespoons finely chopped fresh cilantro, for garnish

Potato chips, for serving

SERVES 8

Make the Dip

Transfer the beans to a medium bowl and cover with boiling water. Let the beans soak until they are warmed through, 10 to 15 minutes. Meanwhile, in a food processor (or blender) add the sour cream, lemon juice, sesame oil, sriracha, garlic, salt, and black pepper and set aside until the beans are ready. Thoroughly drain the beans, then add them to the food processor and blend until smooth, about 60 seconds.

Serve

Transfer to a serving dish and garnish with more sesame oil and sriracha, the olive oil, cilantro, and a few cracks of black pepper. Serve warm alongside your favorite potato chips.

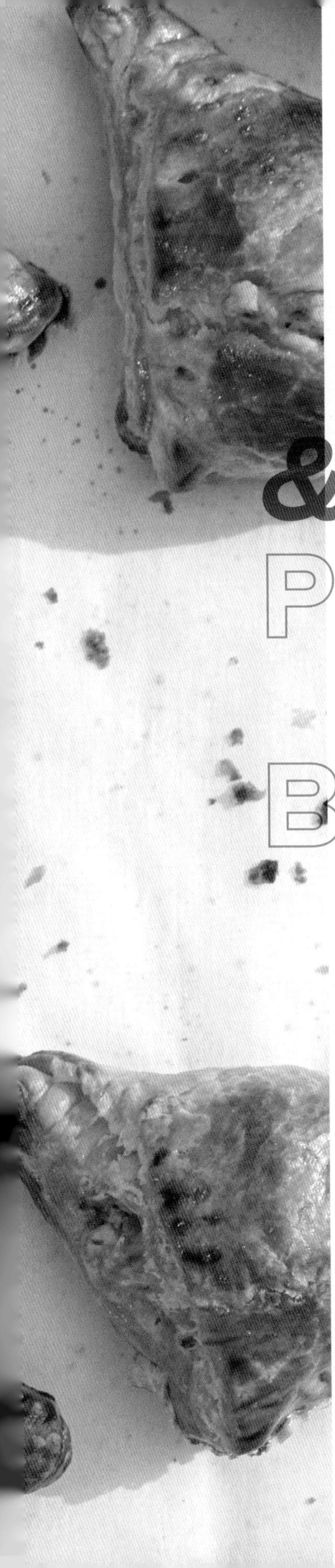

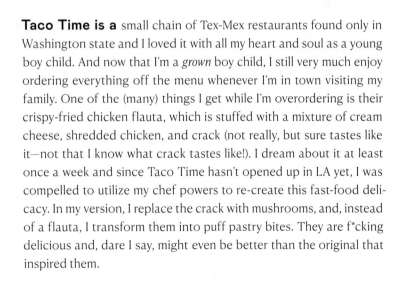

Chicken & Mushroom PUFF PASTRY BITES

Taco Time is a small chain of Tex-Mex restaurants found only in Washington state and I loved it with all my heart and soul as a young boy child. And now that I'm a *grown* boy child, I still very much enjoy ordering everything off the menu whenever I'm in town visiting my family. One of the (many) things I get while I'm overordering is their crispy-fried chicken flauta, which is stuffed with a mixture of cream cheese, shredded chicken, and crack (not really, but sure tastes like it—not that I know what crack tastes like!). I dream about it at least once a week and since Taco Time hasn't opened up in LA yet, I was compelled to utilize my chef powers to re-create this fast-food delicacy. In my version, I replace the crack with mushrooms, and, instead of a flauta, I transform them into puff pastry bites. They are f*cking delicious and, dare I say, might even be better than the original that inspired them.

1 medium bone-in, skin-on chicken thigh (about 7 ounces)

6 to 7 cremini mushrooms (about 3 ounces)

1 tablespoon canola oil

Kosher salt

Freshly ground black pepper

6 ounces (¾ brick) cream cheese, room temperature

3 scallions, dark green parts only, finely chopped

2 cloves garlic, minced

1 (10 x 10-inch) sheet frozen puff pastry, thawed in the fridge overnight

1 large egg, beaten

MAKES 16 BITES

| Roast the Chicken | Position a rack in the center of the oven and preheat the oven to 400°F. Line a small baking dish with parchment paper and arrange the chicken and mushrooms in a single layer. Drizzle with the oil and season with salt and black pepper. Roast until the chicken is cooked through and the mushrooms have shrunk, 30 to 35 minutes. Leave the oven on and let the chicken rest at room temperature for 15 minutes. |

| Make the Filling | Shred the chicken skin and meat, discarding the bone. Transfer the chicken (skin and meat) and mushrooms to a cutting board and chop finely. In a medium bowl, mix together the cream cheese, scallions, garlic, chopped chicken and mushrooms, and any residual juices from the baking dish until thoroughly combined. Transfer to the fridge for 15 to 20 minutes to firm up (this will make it easier to fill the puff pastry). |

| Fill the Puff Pastry | Line a large baking sheet with parchment paper. On a lightly floured surface, use a rolling pin to flatten the puff pastry into a 12-inch square. Using a sharp knife or bench scraper, cut the puff pastry into 16 squares. Place a heaping tablespoon of filling into the center of each square and carefully fold into a triangle (stretching the dough as needed). Pinch along the edges to seal and transfer to the prepared baking sheet, arranging each pastry about ½ inch away apart. |

| Bake the Bites | Using the tines of a fork, crimp the edges of each pocket. Brush the top of each pastry with the beaten egg. Using a sharp paring knife, make a couple of slits on the top of each pastry (so some steam can escape) and bake until they are puffed up and golden brown, 14 to 16 minutes (some filling may ooze out, but that's totally okay!). Transfer to a serving plate and serve warm. |

| Storage | Once cooled, these puff pastry bites can be stored in a large freezer bag and frozen for up to 3 months. When you want to eat them, preheat an oven to 400°F and bake them straight from frozen until heated through and crispy on top, 5 to 7 minutes. |

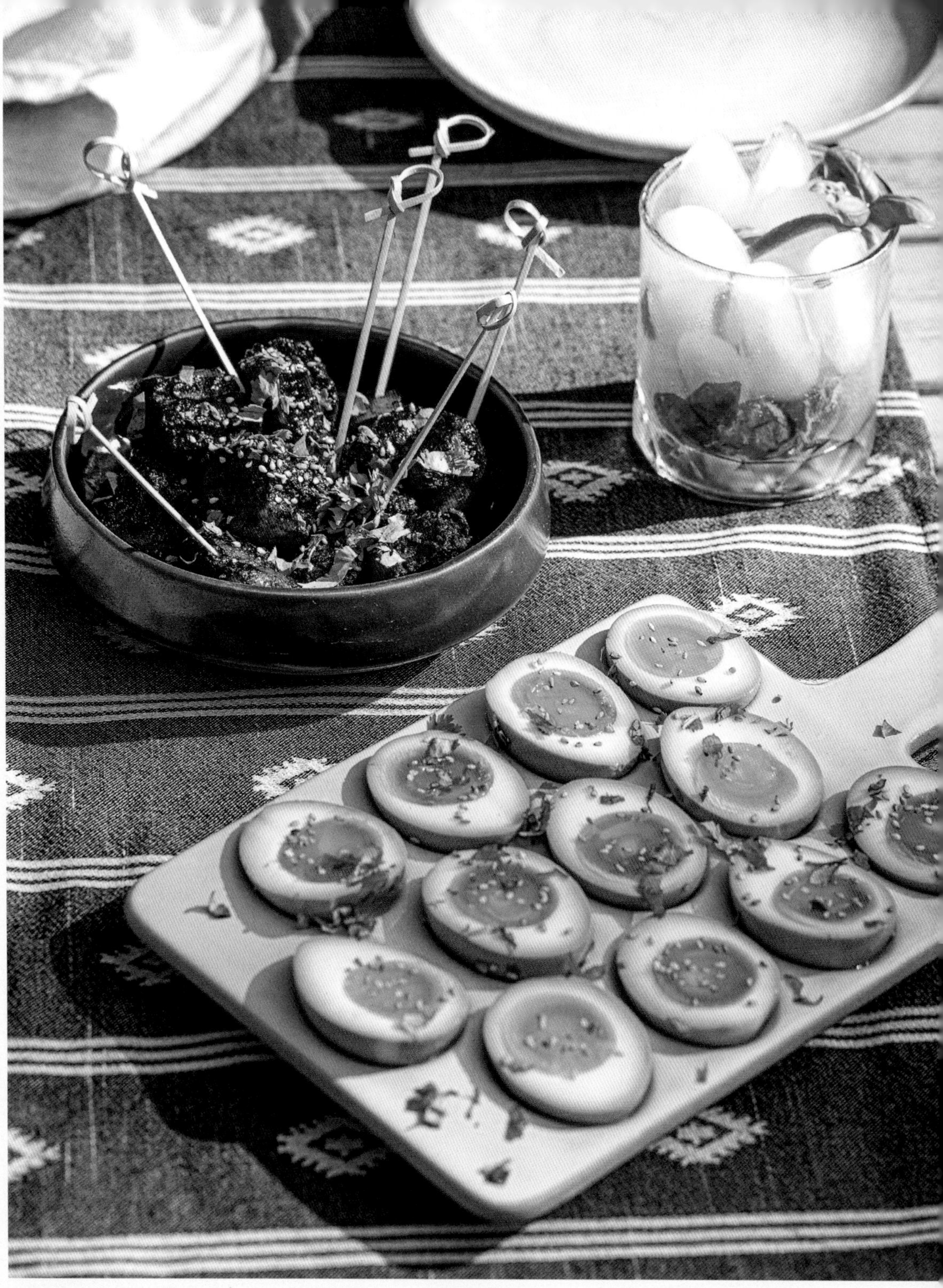

JAMMY
Ramen Eggs
& Sriracha Pork Belly

RAMEN EGGS

6 large eggs

¼ cup reduced-sodium soy sauce

2 tablespoons filtered water

1 tablespoon granulated sugar

1 teaspoon extra virgin olive oil

SRIRACHA PORK BELLY

2 tablespoons reduced-sodium soy sauce

2 tablespoons sriracha

2 tablespoons orange juice

1 teaspoon packed brown sugar (light or dark)

2 cloves garlic, minced

1 pound pork belly, cut into 12 equal pieces

1 to 2 cups chicken stock, beef stock, or water

2 tablespoons finely chopped fresh cilantro, for garnish

Toasted sesame seeds, for garnish

MAKES 12 PIECES EACH

Ramen eggs and pork belly are usually considered add-on toppings at your favorite noodle shop, but I think they deserve more than sidekick status. And contrary to what my mom constantly tells my sisters, having older eggs and a soft belly are not always a bad thing. In fact, slightly older eggs (ones that have been in your fridge for a week or two) will actually yield an easier-to-peel boiled egg. Making jammy ramen eggs is as simple as boiling, peeling, and marinating them, while the sriracha pork belly requires only a quick sauce and a braise before it's transformed into savory, melt-in-your-mouth morsels. These two goodies are the perfect little snack pair for happy hour as is, but, like almost everything else, also absolutely delectable atop a bowl of steaming rice (or ramen, obviously).

Boil the Eggs

Bring a large pot of water to a boil. When the water is boiling, use a slotted spoon (or spider) to carefully lower the eggs into the water. Immediately set the timer for 6½ minutes. Once the timer goes off, transfer the eggs to a bowl and submerge under cold running water for 1 minute.

Peel the Eggs

When the eggs have cooled, gently crack them on a hard surface and slip the shells off under cool running water (which will help to gently separate the shell membrane from the egg white). Transfer the peeled eggs to a large freezer bag.

Marinate the Eggs

In a small bowl, whisk together the soy sauce, water, sugar, and oil until the sugar dissolves. Pour the marinade into the freezer bag and gently roll the eggs around to coat. Squeeze out as much air as possible and seal the bag. Place the bag of eggs in a medium bowl and refrigerate for at least 3 hours, occasionally rotating the bag to marinate the eggs evenly.

Make the Pork Belly

In a small saucepan, whisk together the soy sauce, sriracha, orange juice, brown sugar, and garlic until combined. Add the pork belly and gently toss to coat. Add as much stock as needed to cover the pork belly and bring to a boil. Reduce the heat to a simmer, cover, and cook until the pork belly starts to get tender, about 40 minutes. Remove the lid and continue to cook until it is fork-tender and the liquid is reduced by half, about 25 minutes, stirring occasionally to prevent burning.

| Serve | Transfer the pork belly to a serving bowl. Slice each egg in half lengthwise and transfer to a serving platter. Garnish both dishes with the cilantro and toasted sesame seeds right before serving. |

Make Ahead

The longer you marinate the eggs, the saltier they will get, so I recommend removing them from the marinade after 8 to 10 hours (but feel free to experiment with shorter or longer times depending on your preference). Store them in an airtight container in the fridge for up to 5 days.

CRISPY
Rice Paper Pockets
with Pork & Napa Cabbage ➤

Whenever I go to a Vietnamese restaurant, I place two orders of crispy spring rolls (also known as "cha gio") before my booty even touches the seat. It's my way of letting the restaurant know that I ain't messing around and they better get ready for the bottomless pit that is my stomach. In my opinion, the Vietnamese spring roll is the king of spring rolls. The wrapper is light and uber-crispy while the filling is meaty and satiating. This is my bulkier version of cha gio, which is more like an Asian hot pocket than an egg roll. The filling is made with ground pork, shredded cabbage, and just a little bit of soft tofu. I generally think tofu is pointless, but its addition here really helps keep the filling juicy and tender. To ensure the pockets don't fall apart during cooking, my recipe calls for two layers of rice paper wrappers. And unlike traditional egg rolls, these babies are pan-fried until they develop that delectable crispy exterior while still maintaining a little bit of chewiness from the rice paper. To serve, these crispy meat-filled pockets are wrapped in fresh lettuce and dipped in nuoc cham, resulting in a mouthful that is balanced and utterly delicious.

NUOC CHAM

3 tablespoons fresh lime juice

3 tablespoons fish sauce

2 tablespoons granulated sugar

1 Thai chili, finely chopped, or ½ teaspoon crushed red pepper flakes

FILLING

½ pound ground pork

½ cup soft (or medium-firm) tofu, drained and crumbled

½ cup very finely shredded napa cabbage

2 tablespoons minced chives, fresh or dried

1½ tablespoons soy sauce

1 tablespoon fish sauce

1 tablespoon toasted sesame oil

1 tablespoon granulated sugar

1 tablespoon onion powder

1 tablespoon cornstarch

2 cloves garlic, minced

1 large egg yolk

16 (8-inch) rice paper wrappers

Canola oil, for pan-frying

1 scallion, green parts only, chopped, for garnish

Butter or romaine lettuce leaves, for serving

MAKES 8 POCKETS

Make the Nuoc Cham

In a small bowl, whisk together the lime juice, fish sauce, sugar, chili, and ¼ cup of water until the sugar dissolves. Set aside.

Make the Filling

In a medium bowl, mix the pork, tofu, cabbage, chives, soy sauce, fish sauce, sesame oil, sugar, onion powder, cornstarch, garlic, and egg yolk until fully combined (do not overmix). The mixture should be moist but still hold its shape.

Wrap the Pockets

Fill a pie dish with cold water. Dip a rice paper wrapper in the water and shake off the excess. Place on a large cutting board and add about 3 tablespoons of filling in the center. When the wrapper is pliable, 10 to 15 seconds, fold the bottom third of the wrapper toward the center, followed by the top third and sides to form a square pocket, making sure there are no trapped air bubbles. Moisten another rice paper wrapper and wrap the pocket one more time using the same method. Transfer to a plate and continue with the rest of the filling and wrappers.

Pan-Fry the Pockets

In a large nonstick skillet over medium-high heat, drizzle in a couple of tablespoons of the oil. When the oil is hot, gently place the pockets into the skillet, 1 inch apart, working in batches, if necessary. Pan-fry until the exterior is crispy and golden brown and the filling is cooked through, 5 to 7 minutes on each side. Using tongs, transfer to a serving plate, garnish with the chopped scallions, and serve immediately with the lettuce leaves and nuoc cham sauce.

CRISPY HOT HONEY Baked
Chicken Wings

Through all the ups and downs of life, one thing has never changed and that's my love for chicken wings. When I went through my first breakup, chicken wings were there to comfort me. When I booked my very first modeling job, chicken wings were there to congratulate me (after the photo shoot, of course). And when I got engaged to Doug, we celebrated by binging on chicken wings that very same night. Like a best friend, chicken wings have just always been there for me. I like my chicken wings crispy, saucy, and served with an entirely different sauce so that eating them is deliciously messy. These baked chicken wings check all the right boxes, and thanks to a thin coating of seasoned rice flour, they get extra crispy. After hanging out in the oven for a bit, they're tossed in a garlicky, spicy honey sauce before getting dunked in my Crunchy Corn Onion Dip (page 36). With the ideal crispiness-to-sauce-to-meat ratio, these wings will be there for you no matter the occasion.

CHICKEN WING RUB

3 tablespoons rice flour or cornstarch

2 teaspoons chili powder

2 teaspoons garlic powder

2 teaspoons onion powder

1½ teaspoons kosher salt

1½ teaspoons freshly ground black pepper

3 pounds whole chicken wings, tips removed

Crunchy Corn Onion Dip (page 36), for serving

CHICKEN WING SAUCE

3 tablespoons unsalted butter

3 tablespoons honey

3 tablespoons sambal oelek (kimchi brining liquid or sriracha will work too)

2 tablespoons packed brown sugar (light or brown)

1 tablespoon fish sauce

3 cloves garlic, minced

3 tablespoons finely chopped fresh cilantro, plus more for garnish

Lime wedges (optional), for serving

SERVES 8

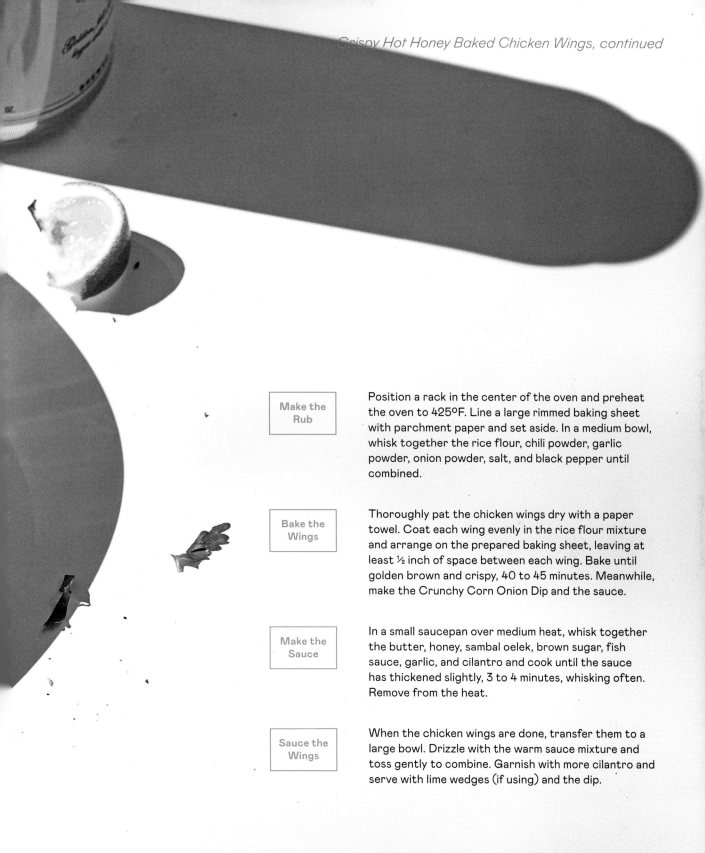

Make the Rub

Position a rack in the center of the oven and preheat the oven to 425°F. Line a large rimmed baking sheet with parchment paper and set aside. In a medium bowl, whisk together the rice flour, chili powder, garlic powder, onion powder, salt, and black pepper until combined.

Bake the Wings

Thoroughly pat the chicken wings dry with a paper towel. Coat each wing evenly in the rice flour mixture and arrange on the prepared baking sheet, leaving at least ½ inch of space between each wing. Bake until golden brown and crispy, 40 to 45 minutes. Meanwhile, make the Crunchy Corn Onion Dip and the sauce.

Make the Sauce

In a small saucepan over medium heat, whisk together the butter, honey, sambal oelek, brown sugar, fish sauce, garlic, and cilantro and cook until the sauce has thickened slightly, 3 to 4 minutes, whisking often. Remove from the heat.

Sauce the Wings

When the chicken wings are done, transfer them to a large bowl. Drizzle with the warm sauce mixture and toss gently to combine. Garnish with more cilantro and serve with lime wedges (if using) and the dip.

Tomato Butter
FLATBREAD with Burrata & Basil

3 tablespoons extra
virgin olive oil,
plus more for
drizzling and
brushing

1 pound cherry
tomatoes

1 tablespoon
unsalted butter

1 tablespoon dried
oregano

1 teaspoon kosher
salt

2 cloves garlic,
minced

8 ounces pizza
dough,
homemade
or store-
bought, room
temperature

8 ounces burrata
cheese

½ cup fresh basil
leaves, roughly
torn

Grated Parmesan
cheese, for
serving

Crushed red pepper
flakes, for
serving

SERVES 6

When I was a kid, my mom would tell me, "This grease is going to clog your arteries and you will die," right before blotting off every last drop of flavor from my pizza. I guess that's why I *thought* I didn't like pizza because (a) it tasted rubbery and dry and (b) apparently cheese grease is poison! Yes, too much grease *might* kill you, but so will *not* eating greasy pizza! That's why these smaller, more approachable versions, a.k.a. flatbreads, are a good compromise. The key is to parbake the dough, which keeps the crust from getting soggy even after all the toppings are added. The tomato "butter" is fresh and intense and can be made with any type of tomatoes, while the chunks of burrata feed my insatiable desire for, well, cheese! I kept this recipe simple, but see it as an open invitation to top the flatbread with anything else your soul desires . . . perhaps more cheese?

Make the Tomato Butter
Position a rack in the top of the oven and preheat the oven to 500°F. In a medium saucepan over medium heat, add the olive oil and tomatoes. Cover and cook until the tomatoes burst and break down, 6 to 7 minutes, stirring occasionally. Add the butter, oregano, salt, and garlic and cook, uncovered, until the sauce has thickened slightly, 5 to 7 minutes, stirring occasionally. Remove from the heat and set aside.

Parbake the Crust
Drizzle a little bit of olive oil over the dough and divide in half. Stretch each piece of dough into a thin, roughly shaped oval about 12 inches long (it doesn't need to be perfect), leaving the edges a little thicker. Transfer to a large rimmed baking sheet and bake until lightly browned and puffy, 3 to 4 minutes.

Assemble the Flatbreads
Brush the edges of each parbaked crust with olive oil and spread half of the tomato butter into an even layer on each one, leaving a ½-inch border on the edge. Bake until the crust is golden brown, 5 to 7 minutes.

Garnish the Flatbreads
Gently tear the burrata into pieces and arrange on top of each flatbread. Garnish with the basil, Parmesan, more olive oil, and pepper flakes. Slice and serve immediately.

Tip

If tomatoes aren't in season and your sauce is just a little bit sour, add a teaspoon of sugar to balance it out.

Crispy Rice
CROSTINI

RICE CROSTINI
Cooking spray

1 cup uncooked white sushi rice, rinsed, soaked for 20 minutes, and drained

2 tablespoons unseasoned rice vinegar

2 teaspoons granulated sugar

½ teaspoon kosher salt

Canola oil, for pan-frying

Topping(s) of choice (recipes follow)

MAKES 16 RICE CROSTINI

Tip

I'm usually all about substitutions, but this is one of those recipes where you have to use white sushi rice. Cooked white sushi rice has a stickier consistency than other types of rice, which is what helps the rice crostini hold their shape.

If my sister Kari likes a certain dish, she has this uncanny ability to make it look like it's the most delectable thing in the entire universe. Her eyes light up, and she makes these funny noises that sound like a cross between a cat purring and a toddler giggling. My crispy rice crostini get her to make those strange sounds without fail. I don't blame her because not only are these crispy-crunchy morsels so much fun to eat, but you also have the option to customize the toppings with whatever you want. In this recipe, I offer my three favorite go-tos (spicy tuna, sriracha lime avocado, and kimchi and shrimp cheese), but the possibilities are endless, so feel free to go balls to the wall with your own topping ideas. If you happen to find yourself making strange animal sounds while eating, just go with it because it means the food is damn good and you're living your best life!

Cook the Rice

Grease an 8 × 8-inch baking pan with cooking spray and set aside. In a small saucepan, bring the rice and 1½ cups of water to a boil. Reduce the heat to a simmer, cover, and cook until the water is absorbed and the rice is tender, about 20 minutes. Turn the heat off and let steam, covered, for 10 minutes. (Alternatively, cook the rice in a rice cooker if you have one.)

Prepare the Rice

While the rice is still hot, mix in the vinegar, sugar, and salt until thoroughly combined. Spread the rice into the prepared baking pan and, using a silicone spatula, press firmly into an even, compact layer. Let cool completely, cover with plastic wrap, and refrigerate until firm, about 4 hours, or overnight. In the meantime, make your topping(s) of choice (see next page).

Crisp Up
the Rice

Once you've prepared your toppings, now it's time to crisp up the rice! Using a silicone spatula, gently loosen the edges of the rice (making sure not to break it) before inverting it onto a cutting board. Using a very sharp knife, cut the sheet of cold rice into 16 equal pieces. In a large nonstick skillet over medium heat, add 2 tablespoons of canola oil. When the oil is hot, swirl it around the pan and, working in batches, add as many rice crostini as you can fit (leaving ½ inch in between each one). Cook until golden brown, 5 to 6 minutes on each side, adding more oil as needed. Transfer to a plate and repeat with the remaining rice crostini.

SPICY TUNA

ENOUGH FOR 16 PIECES

3 tablespoons Quick Spicy Mayo (page 37)

½ pound sushi-grade tuna, finely minced

2 serrano peppers, very thinly sliced

In a medium bowl, mix together the spicy mayo and tuna until thoroughly combined. Divide among the crispy rice crostini and garnish each with a couple of thin slices of serrano pepper right before serving.

SRIRACHA LIME AVOCADO

ENOUGH FOR 16 PIECES

2 large avocados, diced

1 tablespoon fresh lime juice

¼ teaspoon kosher salt

Sriracha, for drizzling

1 lime, quartered and very thinly sliced, for garnish

In a medium bowl, add the avocados, lime juice, and salt and mash with a fork until relatively smooth. Divide among the crispy rice crostini and garnish each with a drizzle of sriracha and a slice of lime right before serving.

KIMCHI & SHRIMP CHEESE

ENOUGH FOR 16 PIECES

2 ounces (¼ brick) cream cheese, softened

½ cup chopped cooked shrimp

½ cup kimchi, chopped

½ cup finely shredded sharp Cheddar cheese

1 tablespoon mayonnaise

1 clove garlic, minced

1 scallion, dark green parts only, very finely chopped

16 fresh cilantro leaves, for garnish

In a food processor, add the cream cheese, shrimp, kimchi, Cheddar, mayonnaise, garlic, and scallion and pulse until thoroughly combined. Divide among the crispy rice crostini and garnish each with a cilantro leaf right before serving.

CRAB CAKE
Pot Stickers ➥

1 cup lump crabmeat
   (preferably
   Dungeness), leg
   and/or claw
   meat, picked
   through for
   shells

¼ cup finely crushed
   butter crackers

¼ cup fresh corn
   (thawed frozen
   corn is fine)

2 tablespoons
   mayonnaise

2 tablespoons
   minced chives
   (fresh or dried)

1 tablespoon fresh
   lemon juice

1 teaspoon reduced-
   sodium soy
   sauce

½ teaspoon freshly
   ground black
   pepper

1 large egg

36 round pot sticker
   wrappers,
   store-bought

1 tablespoon canola
   oil

*MAKES 36 POT
STICKERS*

Tip

*I wouldn't fret too
much about making
the pot stickers look
pretty. The ultimate
goal is to just make
sure all the edges
are sealed because
the wonky-looking
ones will taste just as
delicious as the pretty
ones!*

I swear on my love for Britney Spears that I could eat pot stickers for breakfast, lunch, and dinner and never ever grow tired of them (which is the same way I feel about my Shrimp & Cabbage Shanghai Rice Cakes on page 102). In fact, in some parts of the world, people do eat them around the clock, and I hear these are some of the happiest humans on the planet. Thin layers of tasty dough wrapped around whatever the hell you want. Crispy and golden brown on one side, tender and chewy on the other. You know what else I love? Crab cakes. Every year my family and I go crabbing in the Puget Sound and, regardless of how much crab we actually catch, crab cakes always end up on the menu. So, being the smarty pants that I am, I thought I would combine two of my favorite things by filling dumpling wrappers with a savory mixture of crab, corn, and crushed butter crackers, then pan-frying them until golden brown and crispy. Who says you can't have your (crab) cake and eat it too?

Make the Filling	In a medium bowl, mix together the crabmeat, butter crackers, corn, mayonnaise, chives, lemon juice, soy sauce, black pepper, and egg until thoroughly combined (the mixture will look pretty moist).
Wrap the Pot Stickers	Line a large baking sheet with parchment paper. Take 1 heaping teaspoon of crab filling and place it in the center of a pot sticker wrapper. Using your finger, dab the entire border with water. Starting with one pleat, continue pleating until you reach the other edge, firmly pinching the pleats to seal. It does not need to be perfect! Place the wrapped pot sticker onto the prepared baking sheet and continue filling and wrapping the rest of the pot stickers. If the filling starts to release some liquid and looks kind of soggy, simply drain the liquid and continue.
Pan-Fry the Pot Stickers	In a medium nonstick skillet (with a lid), bring 1 cup of water to a boil over high heat. Reduce the heat to medium, place as many pot stickers as you can fit into the pan (without overcrowding), and cover. Cook until the water is absorbed and the pot stickers are opaque, 4 to 5 minutes, making sure to check at the 2-minute mark. Reduce the heat to medium-low and drizzle in the oil, making sure it's evenly distributed. Cook, uncovered, until the bottoms are crispy and deep golden brown, 4 to 5 minutes. Transfer the pot stickers onto a plate and serve warm with sauce of your choice.
Storage	Uncooked pot stickers freeze well, so go ahead and make a double batch. Place the uncooked pot stickers on a baking sheet and pop them in the freezer, uncovered, for at least 4 hours. When they're firm, transfer them to a large freezer bag, and they'll keep for 3 to 4 months. When you're in the mood for pot stickers, cook them straight from frozen, adding 2 to 3 minutes to the cooking time.

How to Wrap a Pot Sticker

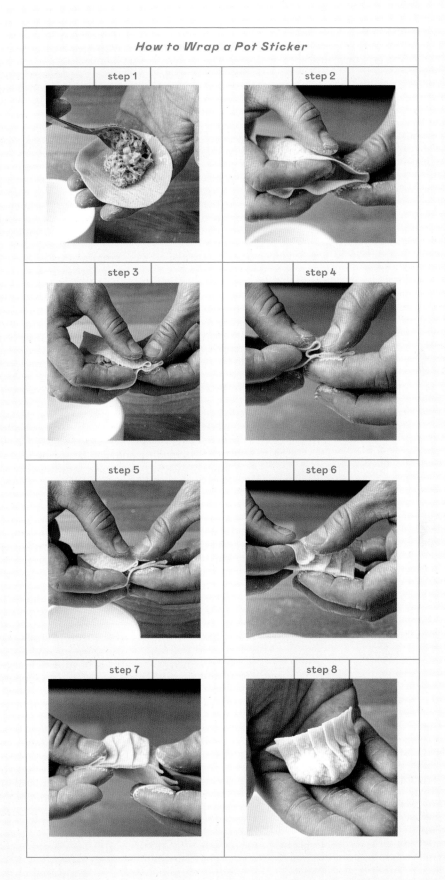

step 1

step 2

step 3

step 4

step 5

step 6

step 7

step 8

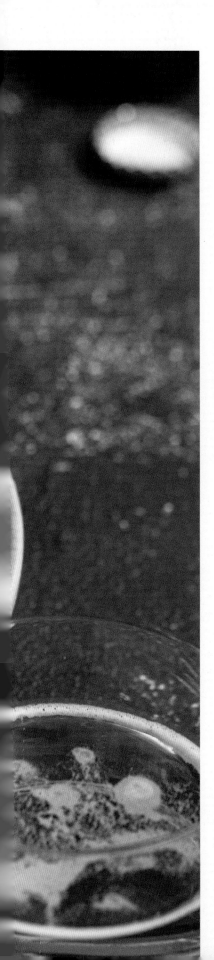

Crispy *Baked* PORK KATSU *Sliders*

Like any good card-carrying chef, I named my dogs after different foods that I love: Taco, Queso, and Unagi. Doug wants to name our next dog Guacamole, but I feel it's a bit of a mouthful to yell when we're trying to get them all to stop harassing the neighborhood squirrel family. Besides, I've already decided that our next dog's name will be Katsu—mainly because I want to shorten it to Kat so I can confuse the hell out of random strangers on our walks when they think I'm calling my dog a cat. But on a more serious note, katsu is one of my favorite Japanese pork dishes. Pork katsu (a.k.a. tonkatsu) is a thinly sliced pork cutlet that gets smothered in panko breadcrumbs, then deep-fried. However, in this recipe, I bake the pork to crispy perfection, top it with a creamy lettuce slaw, and sandwich that sucker between sweet slider rolls and melted cheese for the most delightful snack sandwich you've ever had.

1½ cups panko
     breadcrumbs

4 boneless pork
     chops (about
     1 pound), ½ inch
     thick

½ cup all-purpose
     flour

2 teaspoons kosher
     salt

2 large eggs

3 teaspoons canola
     oil

2 cups very finely
     shredded
     iceberg lettuce

¼ cup mayonnaise,
     plus more for
     toasting rolls

2 tablespoons
     ketchup

1 tablespoon hot
     sauce (I prefer
     Cholula;
     optional)

8 King's Hawaiian or
     brioche slider
     rolls, halved
     widthwise

Shredded mozzarella
     cheese, for
     melting

MAKES 8 SLIDERS

Toast the Panko

Position a rack in the center of the oven and preheat the oven to 400°F. Place an oven-safe wire rack on top of a large rimmed baking sheet and set aside. In a shallow baking dish, spread the panko in an even layer and bake until golden brown, 9 to 10 minutes, tossing halfway through. Remove from the oven and let cool. Leave the oven on.

Prep the Pork

Place the pork chops in a large freezer bag and seal, squeezing out as much air as possible. Using the smooth side of a meat mallet, pound the pork chops until they are about ¼ inch thick. In a medium bowl, whisk together the flour and salt. In another medium bowl, whisk together the eggs and oil until well combined (the oil will help the meat and panko stick better). Take one piece of pork and dredge it in the flour mixture (shaking off any excess), then dip in the egg mixture, and lastly, dredge in the toasted panko (firmly pressing the crumbs into the pork). Transfer to the wire rack–lined baking sheet and repeat with the remaining pork chops. Bake until the pork is cooked through and dark golden brown, 12 to 14 minutes. While the pork is baking, make the slaw and prep the rolls.

Make the Lettuce Slaw

In a medium bowl, toss together the lettuce, mayonnaise, ketchup, and hot sauce (if using) until combined (it will be very saucy).

Prep the Rolls

Spread a thin layer of mayonnaise on each cut side of the rolls. In a large nonstick skillet over medium-low heat, place the bottom half of the rolls cut side down and toast until golden brown, 2 to 3 minutes. Remove the toasted rolls and make 8 little piles of shredded mozzarella on the skillet. Place the top halves of the rolls cut side down directly on top of the cheese and cook until the cheese is completely melted and stuck to the rolls, 45 to 60 seconds.

Assemble the Sliders

When the pork is ready, slice each piece in half. Place a piece of crispy pork on the bottom half of each roll, top with some lettuce slaw, and finish with the melty-cheesy half of the roll. Serve immediately.

California Roll *Sushi Bake* HAND ROLLS

SUSHI RICE

1 cup uncooked white sushi rice, rinsed, soaked for 20 minutes, and drained

2 tablespoons unseasoned rice vinegar

2 teaspoons granulated sugar

½ teaspoon kosher salt

FILLING

12 ounces imitation or real crab, shredded

½ cup mayonnaise or Kewpie Japanese mayonnaise

2 tablespoons tobiko (seasoned flying fish roe), plus more for serving

1 teaspoon unseasoned rice vinegar

½ teaspoon granulated sugar

2 scallions, dark green parts only, very finely chopped

Furikake seasoning, for garnish (optional)

TOPPINGS

10 full-size yaki nori sheets (roasted seaweed wrappers), halved lengthwise

3 Persian cucumbers or ½ English cucumber, cut into 5-inch matchsticks

2 medium avocados, sliced

Soy sauce, for serving (optional)

Wasabi paste, for serving (optional)

Pickled sushi ginger, for serving (optional)

MAKES ABOUT 20 HAND ROLLS

Make Ahead

The rice and crab filling can be assembled a day in advance, covered with plastic wrap, and stored in the fridge. When you're ready for it, transfer the dish directly into a preheated oven and continue with the recipe.

There's a sushi bar in Los Angeles called KazuNori that is dedicated exclusively to hand rolls. What makes this place especially good is that each roll is prepared right in front of you and meant to be devoured straightaway. The combination of the warm filling and the crackly seaweed wrapper makes for an orgasmic experience unlike any other. The problem is that they don't offer a California hand roll. I know a California roll technically isn't even real sushi, but I don't care. It tastes super yummy, and that's what matters to me. So, I've taken matters into my own hands and created something that fills the hole in my stomach for a freshly made California hand roll and, damn, does it fill it good. This recipe calls for simply adding cooked sushi rice to a baking dish, topping it with a creamy mixture of crab, mayonnaise, and scallions, and baking until it's hot and ready. For additional flavor and crunch, I sprinkle on some furikake, a sweet-and-salty blend of sesame seeds and seaweed (find it online or at a local Asian grocery store). The final step to culinary nirvana is to take a crispy nori wrapper, top it with some creamy crab, warm sushi rice, avocado, and cucumber . . . and just go to town. You might be surprised at how many rolls you end up shoving into your face, but if you're anything like me, you will feel zero shame about it.

Cook the Rice	Position a rack in the center of the oven and preheat the oven to 450°F. In a small saucepan, bring the rice and 1½ cups of water to a boil. Reduce the heat to a simmer, cover, and cook until the water is absorbed and the rice is tender, about 20 minutes. Turn the heat off and let steam, covered, for 10 minutes. (Alternatively, cook the rice in a rice cooker if you have one.)
Prepare the Rice	While the rice is still hot, mix in the vinegar, sugar, and salt until thoroughly combined. Evenly spread the rice into an 8 × 8-inch baking dish and set aside.
Make the Filling	In a medium bowl, combine the imitation crab, mayonnaise, tobiko, vinegar, sugar, and scallions. Spread the mixture evenly on top of the rice and bake until slightly browned on the edges, 16 to 18 minutes.
Assemble the Hand Rolls	Garnish the sushi bake with furikake (if using) and serve warm with the nori sheets, cucumbers, avocado, and if using, the soy sauce, wasabi, and pickled ginger on the side. To assemble, take a piece of nori, add a scoop of the sushi bake, and finish it with your desired toppings. Roll it up and eat immediately. To keep the nori wrappers crispy, assemble each hand roll right before you eat it.

CHEESY BEEFY *Pan-Fried* STEAMED BAO ➦

These babies are my bigger and bulkier interpretation of the iconic Shanghainese street food sheng jian bao, which are filled bao that get pan-fried and steamed at the same time, resulting in soft, fluffy buns with crispy bottoms. I like to stuff my buns with a juicy, cheesy beef filling (instead of the traditional fatty pork) because meat + cheese = *never* a bad idea. Plus, the filling also doubles as a recipe for the juiciest meatballs you will ever have in your life. In fact, these stuffed buns are so insanely good that even my very picky niblings (the silly-sounding gender-neutral term for the children of your sibling), Addie, Charlotte, and Levi, will all wait patiently like little angels for the chance to gobble up as many as they can fit into their little tummies. To ensure the bao are tender, I use a simple Asian technique called tangzhong that involves cooking some of the flour and milk together to form a starchy paste before adding it to the rest of the ingredients. This little trick produces dough that absorbs more water and is easier to handle, so the bao are extra pillowy. The only (mildly) tricky part is not burning the bao when pan-frying, so just make sure you keep an eye on them when cooking.

TANGZHONG

¼ cup whole milk

2 tablespoons all-purpose flour

DOUGH

1¼ cups all-purpose flour, plus more for dusting

1¼ teaspoons instant yeast (a.k.a. "fast-rising" or "rapid-rise")

½ teaspoon baking powder

¼ cup whole milk, slightly warmed

2 tablespoons honey

| Make the Tangzhong | In a small saucepan, whisk together the milk, 2 tablespoons of water, and the flour until smooth. Cook over medium heat until it resembles a thick paste (like toothpaste), 2 to 3 minutes, whisking continuously (do not overcook). Scrape into a small bowl and transfer to the fridge until cool, 8 to 10 minutes. |

| Make the Dough | In the bowl of a stand mixer fitted with the dough hook attachment, combine the flour, yeast, and baking powder. Add the milk, honey, and cooled tangzhong and mix on medium-low speed until a smooth, elastic dough forms and pulls away from the sides of the bowl. If needed, add more flour, 1 teaspoon at a time, until the dough no longer sticks. (If you don't have a stand mixer, mix the ingredients in a large bowl until a shaggy dough forms, then scrape out onto a clean surface and knead until smooth and elastic.) Shape the dough into a ball, return it to the bowl, and cover tightly with plastic wrap. Let the dough rise in a warm spot until doubled in size, about 1 hour. Meanwhile, make the filling. |

Tips

If you're using active dry yeast (instead of instant yeast), you will need to rehydrate it first. Just mix the active dry yeast in the warm milk, let sit for 10 minutes until it gets foamy, and then continue with the rest of the instructions.

If you aren't in the mood to make the dough, store-bought fresh pizza dough makes for a great substitute.

Make the Filling	In a large bowl, combine the milk, mayonnaise, and bread and let soak for 5 minutes. Using a fork, mash the mixture until it forms a paste. Add the mozzarella, scallions, soy sauce, cornstarch, brown sugar, and black pepper and mix until thoroughly combined. Add the ground beef and mix until just combined (do not overmix). The filling will look wet and somewhat sticky. Transfer to the fridge until ready to use.
Fill the Bao	Grease a medium nonstick skillet (with a tight-fitting lid) with the oil and set aside. When the dough has doubled in size, scrape it out onto a clean (unfloured) surface and knead until it is smooth. Divide the dough into 8 pieces and shape each piece into a ball. Sprinkle a little flour over each ball and, using a rolling pin, roll each into a 4-inch round. (Tip: I like to use a clean, empty spice jar filled with all-purpose flour to easily dust the dough.) Place about 2 tablespoons of the cheesy beef filling into the center of each round and gently pull the edges up toward the center, pinching firmly together to seal. The bao don't need to be picture-perfect; they just need to be sealed. As you make them, snuggle the sealed buns (pleated side-up) into the prepared skillet.
Cook the Bao	Transfer the bao-filled skillet to the stovetop and cook over medium-low heat until the bao are light golden brown on the bottom, 3 to 4 minutes. Carefully add 1 cup of lukewarm water to the pan and immediately cover with the lid. Cook until all the water has just evaporated and the bao are puffed up, 10 to 13 minutes (check at the 10-minute mark). Remove the lid and cook until the bottoms are crispy and golden brown, an additional 2 to 3 minutes (keep an eye on them so they don't burn). Invert onto a serving plate (crispy side up) and serve immediately.
Storage	Store any leftover bao in an airtight container in the fridge for up to 3 days. When you want to eat one, microwave it for 30 to 45 seconds, until warm. Alternatively, you can wrap them tightly in plastic wrap and freeze for up to 3 months. Thaw in the fridge overnight and microwave for 30 to 45 seconds, until warm.

FILLING

2 tablespoons whole milk

2 tablespoons mayonnaise

½ slice white bread, chopped

½ cup shredded mozzarella cheese

1 scallion, light and dark green parts only, finely chopped

1 tablespoon reduced-sodium soy sauce

1 teaspoon cornstarch

1 teaspoon packed brown sugar (light or dark)

¼ teaspoon freshly ground black pepper

¼ pound ground beef (preferably 80% lean)

1 tablespoon canola oil

MAKES 8 MEDIUM BAO

How to Make and Fill the Bao

step 1

step 2

step 3

step 4

step 5

step 6

step 7

step 8

step 9

Eat Your Veggies

Honey Sriracha Roasted BRUSSELS SPROUTS

with Cashews

1 tablespoon canola oil

1 tablespoon unsalted butter, melted

1 tablespoon fish sauce

1 teaspoon honey, plus more for drizzling

1 teaspoon sriracha, plus more for drizzling

2 cloves garlic, minced

12 ounces brussels sprouts, each sprout cut into 8 wedges

½ cup raw cashews, roughly chopped

SERVES 4

I'll admit that I wasn't always a fan of brussels sprouts. Hell, I didn't even know how to correctly spell *brussels sprouts* until I was today years old! And my mom never made them when I was a kid because we were more of a bok choy kind of family (fun fact: brussels sprouts and bok choy are actually related). Anyway, one day I saw a very, very serious article titled "What Jennifer Lopez Eats in a Day," revealing that she eats brussels sprouts once a week. And ever since that wake-up call, I now also eat brussels sprouts. My favorite way to prepare them is roasted with honey, sriracha, and cashews. Cutting the brussels sprouts into thin wedges is my trick to getting a buttload of crispy, golden-brown edges that transform this humble vegetable into something delectable and flavorful. And although I'm quite a few brussels sprouts away from looking like J.Lo, there's no reason why this journey can't also be delicious.

Make the Sauce

Position a rack in the center of the oven and preheat the oven to 425°F. Line a large rimmed baking sheet with parchment paper. In a medium bowl, whisk together the oil, melted butter, fish sauce, honey, sriracha, and garlic until combined. Add the brussels sprouts and, using your hands, firmly massage the sauce into the sprouts, making sure they are thoroughly coated.

Roast the Brussels Sprouts

Spread the brussels sprouts in an even layer on the prepared baking sheet and roast until tender, 8 to 10 minutes. Add the cashews and toss to combine. Spread everything back into an even layer and roast until the brussels sprouts have crispy edges and the cashews are toasted, 10 to 15 more minutes. Transfer to a serving dish and garnish with more honey and sriracha before serving.

Parmesan-Caramelized BROCCOLI

with Lemon

½ pound broccoli florets (about 3 cups), cut into bite-size pieces

3 tablespoons grated Parmesan cheese

3 tablespoons extra virgin olive oil

2 cloves garlic, minced

¼ teaspoon crushed red pepper flakes

¼ teaspoon kosher salt

1 teaspoon lemon zest

SERVES 2

We eat an exorbitant amount of broccoli at our house, and every time I make this recipe Doug inevitably exclaims, "You make the best broccoli ever!" as if he hasn't tasted it a bazillion times before. Half of me hears a sweet compliment, while the other half questions everything else I've ever cooked for him in my entire life. Turns out Doug might be on to something because everyone else who has tried this recipe also proclaims that it's the best broccoli they've ever eaten. Come to think of it, this recipe yields broccoli that is caramelized, lemony, and cheesy—which essentially makes each floret a flavor bomb for your mouth. The funny part is that all of this takes only a few simple ingredients and a few minutes of your time. Could this *actually* be the "best broccoli ever"?

| Prep the Broccoli | Position a rack in the center of the oven and preheat the oven to 425°F. Line a large rimmed baking sheet with parchment paper. In a large bowl, toss the broccoli, Parmesan, oil, garlic, pepper flakes, and salt until combined, making sure the broccoli gets fully coated in all the ingredients. |

| Roast the Broccoli | Spread the broccoli in an even layer onto the prepared baking sheet and roast until tender and the bottoms are deep golden brown, 14 to 16 minutes. Garnish with the lemon zest and serve immediately. |

Spicy, Vinegary
Shaved Persian Cucumber
SALAD

¼ cup unseasoned rice vinegar

1 tablespoon extra virgin olive oil

1 teaspoon fish sauce

1 teaspoon reduced-sodium soy sauce

1 teaspoon granulated sugar

1 teaspoon crushed red pepper flakes (optional)

6 to 7 Persian cucumbers, shaved into ribbons with a vegetable peeler

1 scallion, dark green parts only, finely chopped

2 tablespoons finely chopped fresh cilantro

Toasted sesame seeds, for garnish

SERVES 2

When I first moved to LA to become a model, I was nineteen years old and poor as a church mouse. Thankfully, my great-godfather lived just outside the city and let me crash with him while I settled into my new SoCal life. He had recently remarried, and his new wife was a charming, sweet, and all-around fantastic human. What I remember most about her, though, was that she had a thing for cucumbers. She was always gnawing on a giant cuke, no matter the time of day. At first I thought it was kind of weird, but she later told me it was her secret to good skin (and, to her credit, she did have amazing skin). From that day on, I became a cucumber convert. However, rather than nibbling away on a whole cucumber every day, I opt to make this refreshing shaved cucumber salad. It's easy to throw together, and I find that letting the cucumbers marinate in the fridge with the vinaigrette allows the flavors to really develop without losing that pleasing crunch. These vinegary strands of crunchy cukes are a great complement to just about any dish, but my favorite thing to do is tuck them into a sandwich or taco (like my Broiled Lamb Tacos with Paprika Lime Sour Cream on page 242).

In a large bowl, whisk together the vinegar, oil, fish sauce, soy sauce, sugar, and pepper flakes (if using) until the sugar dissolves. Add the cucumbers, scallion, and cilantro and toss to combine. Transfer to a freezer bag, squeezing out as much air as possible, and marinate overnight in the fridge (for maximum flavor). Alternatively, transfer to a serving dish, garnish with toasted sesame seeds, and serve immediately.

BABY BOK CHOY

with Pancetta & Scallions

1 teaspoon fish sauce

1 teaspoon toasted sesame oil

2 scallions, light and dark green parts only, chopped

2 cloves garlic, minced

2 ounces pancetta or bacon, chopped

4 to 6 heads baby bok choy (depending on size), halved lengthwise

SERVES 2

Baby bok choy is one of my favorite vegetables—not just because its name is all cutesy, but because this cruciferous "bundle of choy" delivers a juicy, succulent crunch from its hearty stems while its big leafy greens are sweet and delicate. Although *bok choy* means "white vegetable" in Cantonese, *baby* bok choy is harvested earlier, when it is sweeter, more tender, and light green in color. My favorite way to prepare baby bok choy is to cut the heads in half before giving them a super-quick sauté with a teeny bit of rendered pancetta fat and some simple aromatics, like garlic and scallions. The tender leaves wilt ever so slightly and the stems stay nice and crunchy. This recipe is so tasty that I promise you'll be "bok" for more! I also promise no more cringey vegetable puns.

Make the Sauce

In a small bowl, whisk together the fish sauce, sesame oil, scallions, garlic, and 2 tablespoons of water and set aside.

Cook the Pancetta

In a large skillet or wok over medium heat, add the pancetta and cook until the fat has rendered and the pancetta is golden brown, 3 to 4 minutes.

Cook the Bok Choy

Add the prepared sauce and baby bok choy to the skillet and toss to combine. Arrange the bok choy cut side down in an even layer and cook until the leafy green parts have wilted but the white parts still have a subtle crunch, 3 to 4 minutes. Transfer the bok choy, pancetta, and any residual sauce to a serving plate. Serve immediately.

Asparagus & Chorizo
STIR-FRY

½ pound Mexican-style chorizo or spicy Italian sausage, casings removed

Canola oil, as needed

1 pound asparagus, trimmed and cut on a diagonal into 2-inch pieces

2 cloves garlic, minced

SERVES 4

When I was growing up, my mom always tried to sell my sisters and me on all the benefits of eating vegetables, as if little twats like us really cared about vitamins and minerals. We were invincible! Since my mom isn't a dumb lady (and was in charge of all our meals), she knew exactly how to get us to eat our veggies—and that was by adding just enough meat to lure us into a vegetable-centric dish. Sorry, vegetarians, but this method only works for us bar-barians. Although, for the record, I've gotten to a point in my life where I actually just enjoy eating vegetables, thank you very much! That said, I still love some meat with my veggies, and this asparagus-chorizo stir-fry is the perfect meat-to-vegetable marriage. The best part is that since the chorizo is already so flavorful and the ingredients are minimal, this dish comes together in a flash.

Tip
Make sure you buy the Mexican-style chorizo (which is raw) for this recipe and not the Spanish-style chorizo (which is cured).

Brown the Chorizo

In a large skillet or wok over medium heat, cook the chorizo until browned, 5 to 6 minutes, breaking up any large chunks with a wooden spatula. If needed, add a tablespoon of canola oil to help with the browning, but since most chorizo is pretty fatty, you probably won't need it.

Cook the Asparagus

Add the asparagus, garlic, and ¼ cup of water and toss to combine. Increase the heat to medium-high and cook until the asparagus is just tender and the water evaporates, 4 to 6 minutes (depending on the thickness of the stalks), occasionally loosening any browned bits on the bottom of the skillet with the spatula. Transfer to a serving plate and serve immediately.

Citrus Soy *Shishito Peppers* with Garlic Panko

¼ cup panko
    breadcrumbs

1 tablespoon extra
    virgin olive oil

1 clove garlic, minced

2 teaspoons
    reduced-sodium
    soy sauce

2 teaspoons fresh
    orange juice

2 teaspoons fresh
    lemon juice

2 teaspoons fresh
    lime juice

½ pound shishito
    peppers

1 tablespoon canola
    oil

SERVES 2

Tip

Toasted panko is also fantastic sprinkled over any salad or pasta for an added crunch. Unlike big chunky stale croutons whose only purpose in life is to cut up the inside of your mouth, toasted panko would never even think of doing that. And because they are little crumbs, you get an even distribution of yummy crunch in every bite.

Roughly one in ten shishito peppers will hit you with a tongue-tingling kick, which makes for a really fun game of Russian roulette but without anyone dying (which is always a good thing). Shishito peppers actually taste kind of bland when they're raw, but if they frolic around in a hot skillet and start to blister and char, they will transform into something that your mouth is happy to receive. As soon as the peppers develop that subtle, smoky char, hit them with a salty-tangy-sweet citrus soy sauce and cover them with crunchy toasted panko breadcrumbs. All you have left to do now is just pop the entire pepper (except the stem) into your yapper and, depending on whether you want some excitement, hope you get a spicy one.

Toast the Panko	In a small skillet over medium-low heat, combine the panko and olive oil and cook until light golden brown, 4 to 5 minutes, stirring continuously. The panko burns easily, so make sure to constantly move it around the pan. Remove from the heat, add the garlic, and toss until combined. Leave the panko in the pan until needed.
Cook the Shishitos	In a small bowl, whisk together the soy sauce, citrus juices, and 2 teaspoons of water until combined. In a large bowl, toss together the shishito peppers and canola oil until the peppers are evenly coated in oil. In a large cast-iron skillet over medium heat, add the oiled peppers and cook, undisturbed, until they begin to "puff up" and char, 2 to 3 minutes on each side. Add the soy sauce mixture and toss continuously until everything is hot, 45 to 60 seconds.
Serve	Transfer the shishito peppers to a serving dish and garnish with the garlic panko. Serve immediately.

CRISPY
Mushrooms
with Soy & Pecorino

3 ounces shiitake mushrooms, stemmed and halved

3 ounces trumpet mushrooms, cut into bite-size chunks

2 ounces oyster mushrooms, halved

2 ounces maitake mushrooms, separated into bite-size clusters

3 tablespoons grated Pecorino Romano cheese (pregrated works great for this), plus more for garnish

2 tablespoons canola oil

2 teaspoons reduced-sodium soy sauce

1 teaspoon toasted sesame oil

SERVES 2

A while back my best friend was dating a guy who openly admitted to hating mushrooms, and I couldn't help but feel personally attacked. What kind of human being doesn't love mushrooms? There was no way I was going to allow my dear friend to be with such a monster, so needless to say, he's no longer with us. And just to clarify, he's still alive, just not *with* us. For all the awesome people who do love mushrooms, this recipe is super exciting because it uses a variety of fungi that offer different textures and flavors! And who wouldn't want to feast on a dish comprised entirely of mushrooms that are meaty, crispy, and juicy all at the same time? Oh yeah, someone who wants to be dumped.

Tip

Wash or wipe? I can't answer that question when it comes to your personal hygiene, but I can in regard to mushrooms. If you want them to be crispy (like in this recipe), brush off any dirt with a clean toothbrush designated for culinary purposes only, then wipe them clean with a dry paper towel. For all the other times, just give them a quick scrub and rinse under cool running water.

Roast the Mushrooms

Position a rack in the center of the oven and preheat the oven to 425°F. Line a large rimmed baking sheet with parchment paper (and, yes, it has to be parchment paper for this recipe). In a large bowl, gently toss together the mushrooms, Pecorino Romano, canola oil, soy sauce, and sesame oil until the mushrooms are thoroughly coated. Transfer to the prepared baking sheet and spread into an even layer. Roast until browned on the bottom, 14 to 16 minutes. Flip the mushrooms and roast until crispy, another 7 to 8 minutes.

Serve

Transfer the mushrooms to a serving dish and sprinkle with more grated Pecorino Romano. Serve immediately.

Cauliflower "Polenta"

2 pounds cauliflower florets (about 6 cups), cut into 2-inch pieces

1¼ cups half-and-half, plus more as needed

½ teaspoon kosher salt

¾ cup grated Pecorino Romano cheese, plus more for garnish

3 tablespoons unsalted butter

2 teaspoons freshly ground black pepper, plus more for garnish

Extra virgin olive oil, for drizzling

SERVES 8

Honesty is the most important thing in any healthy relationship, and I have to be honest with you—this subbing cauliflower-for-carbs trend needs to stop! The simple truth is cauliflower isn't bread, and no matter how hard you try, it never will be. Cauliflower pizza crust? That's just dried-up mush. Cauliflower nachos? It ain't nachos without the tortilla chips. Cauliflower rice? Now that's just straight-up disrespectful. However, I will admit that there is one, and only one, carb substitute that actually works, and it is my Cacio e Pepe Cauliflower "Polenta." Salty Pecorino Romano, freshly cracked black pepper, and creamy cooked cauliflower are blended together to create a side dish that doesn't feel or taste like it's trying to be something it's not. Because unlike the other carb impersonators, this one scratches that itch for a hot, cheesy, stick-to-your-ribs porridge without having to pretend it tastes good . . . because it actually *does*.

Cook the Cauliflower

In a large pot over medium-high heat, add the cauliflower, half-and-half, and salt and bring to a boil. Immediately reduce the heat to a simmer, cover, and cook until the cauliflower is very tender (but not mushy), 6 to 8 minutes. Remove from the heat and let cool for 5 to 10 minutes.

Blend the Ingredients

Transfer the cauliflower mixture to a food processor (or blender) along with the Pecorino Romano, butter, and black pepper and blend until you reach a grainy consistency, 3 to 5 pulses, adding more half-and-half as needed. If you want more of a puree consistency, blend until the mixture is smooth. If you accidentally add too much half-and-half, return the mixture to the pot and simmer until you reach your desired consistency.

Serve

Transfer to a serving dish and garnish with more Pecorino Romano, black pepper, and a drizzle of olive oil. Serve immediately.

Blistered
MISO BUTTER GREEN BEANS
with Crispy Fried Onions

1 tablespoon unsalted butter, melted

1 tablespoon yellow or white miso paste

1 scallion, light and dark green parts only, finely chopped

1 clove garlic, minced

1 pound green beans, trimmed

2 tablespoons canola oil

½ teaspoon kosher salt

¼ cup crispy fried onions (such as French's), for garnish

SERVES 4

If I were a magical fairy, I would spend my time wandering around town sprinkling crispy fried onions onto people's food . . . right before fluttering away with a toothy grin and a sparkle in my eye knowing that I made someone's day just a little bit yummier. I would obviously ask them first because it's not cool to put things in people's food without their consent. I just love crispy fried onions because when used properly they can turn something good into something great—and these blistered miso butter green beans are no exception. This recipe is my very, very, very loose take on a green bean casserole, just without the whole casserole part. So, I guess when I say loose, I mean it's nothing like it. These slightly charred green beans are damn delectable all on their own, but at the risk of sounding like a flavor-obsessed drama queen, the addition of the crispy fried onions makes these the best goddamn green beans you will ever eat.

Make the Sauce	Position a rack in the center of the broiler and preheat the broiler to high. In a small bowl, whisk together the melted butter, miso paste, scallion, garlic, and 1 tablespoon of water until combined. Set aside.
Blister the Green Beans	In a large bowl, toss together the green beans, oil, and salt until the beans are thoroughly coated. Spread the beans in an even layer onto a large rimmed baking sheet and broil until charred in some spots, 4 to 5 minutes.
Serve	As soon as the beans come out of the oven, pour the prepared sauce over them and toss until thoroughly combined. Transfer to a serving dish and garnish with crispy fried onions. Serve immediately.

CRISPY

Salt & Vinegar *Roasted Potatoes* with Parmesan

2 pounds russet
   or Yukon Gold
   potatoes,
   scrubbed and
   cut into 1-inch
   pieces

1 teaspoon baking
   soda

2 tablespoons kosher
   salt

¼ cup canola oil

2 tablespoons
   distilled white
   vinegar

2 tablespoons finely
   chopped fresh
   flat-leaf parsley

2 cloves garlic,
   minced

Grated Parmesan
   cheese, for
   garnish

SERVES 4

Make Ahead

You can prep (boil, season, and toss) the potatoes in advance and store them covered in plastic wrap in the fridge for up to 3 days. When you need them, just transfer the prepped potatoes to a parchment paper–lined baking sheet and pop them straight into a preheated oven.

Personally, I like my potato morsels crispy and crunchy on the outside but creamy and soft on the inside. If that sounds like your kind of spud, this is the recipe for you. The secret to making these potatoes is boiling them first, before roughing them up a little bit like they owe you money. That way, a thin layer of starch forms and crisps up in the oven while the insides of the potatoes remain all buttery and smooth. With just a subtle hint of vinegar, parsley, and garlic, these perfect little bite-size tater chunks are everything you need and want, whether as a side dish or your new best friend . . . that you happen to eat . . . at midnight.

Boil the Potatoes

Position a rack in the center of the oven and preheat the oven to 450°F. Line a large rimmed baking sheet with parchment paper and set aside. In a large pot, add the potatoes, baking soda, and salt. Fill with just enough water to cover the potatoes and bring to a boil. Immediately reduce the heat to a simmer and cook until the potatoes are just tender, 11 to 13 minutes (from the time you start simmering). Do not overcook the potatoes or they will fall apart when you toss them. In the meantime, make the sauce.

Make the Sauce

In a small saucepan over medium-high heat, combine the oil, vinegar, parsley, and garlic and cook until the garlic is fragrant, about 1 minute. Remove from the heat and set aside.

Toss the Potatoes

Drain the potatoes in a colander and let them sit for 2 to 3 minutes so the excess moisture can evaporate. Transfer the potatoes to a large bowl along with the vinegar mixture. Using your hands, gently toss the potatoes until they are coated with a thin layer of starch (it will look kind of lumpy).

Roast the Potatoes

Spread the potatoes in an even layer onto the prepared baking sheet and roast until deep golden brown and crispy, 35 to 45 minutes, tossing them halfway through. Sprinkle with grated Parmesan while still warm and serve immediately.

Brown Butter
EGGPLANT ADOBO
with Roasted Peanuts

¼ cup unseasoned rice vinegar or distilled white vinegar

2 tablespoons yellow or white miso paste

2 tablespoons reduced-sodium soy sauce

2 tablespoons honey or maple syrup

½ teaspoon ground white pepper

2 tablespoons unsalted butter

¼ cup extra virgin olive oil, plus more as needed

1 pound Japanese or Chinese eggplants, cut into bite-size chunks

2 tablespoons unsalted roasted peanuts, roughly chopped

SERVES 4

Could you imagine if there were rumors flying around that you were bitter and had no personality, and, to top it off, you were always being called a d*ck? Now you know what an eggplant feels like! To help put a stop to these lies, here are a few pointers that will turn these adorable purple ding-a-lings into a delicious, melt-in-your-mouth delicacy. First, eggplants require a healthy amount of oil to achieve the tender, silky creaminess that makes them so delectable. Second, I used to salt my eggplant prior to cooking before I realized that it didn't really make a difference, so I stopped doing it altogether. Lastly, stick to smaller eggplants because the larger ones actually do become bitter and tend to have tougher, less appetizing skin—in this case, bigger isn't *always* better. Now that you have your facts straight, my eggplant adobo recipe will have you falling in love with the misunderstood aubergine in no time. Thanks to the rice vinegar, miso paste, soy sauce, and honey, this dish hits every taste bud on your tongue in the best way possible. This recipe is one of my favorite ways to prepare eggplant, and while it's great as a side dish, it's even better as the main (served with a big bowl of steaming rice, of course).

Make the Sauce

In a small bowl, whisk together the vinegar, miso, soy sauce, honey, white pepper, and 1 cup of water until smooth. In a large skillet over low heat, melt the butter and cook until the milk solids begin to brown, 3 to 4 minutes. Carefully pour the browned butter into the sauce mixture and whisk until fully combined. Set aside.

Cook the Eggplant

In the same large skillet over medium heat, add the olive oil. When the oil is hot, add the eggplant and cook until browned, 3 to 4 minutes on each side, adding more oil as needed to keep the skillet greased. The eggplant will absorb a good bit of the oil and will also begin to char a little. Add the sauce mixture, scraping the bottom of the skillet with a wooden spatula to loosen any browned bits. Bring to a simmer and cook until the eggplant is tender and the sauce has been mostly absorbed, about 25 minutes, occasionally shaking the skillet to prevent burning.

Serve

Transfer to a serving dish and garnish with crushed peanuts. Serve immediately.

Frickin' Chicken

ANYTHING-
BUT-BASIC

Roasted
Chicken Broth

1 whole chicken
(3½ to
4½ pounds)

1 tablespoon canola
oil

Kosher salt

Freshly ground black
pepper

1 large onion,
unpeeled and
rinsed well,
roots removed,
cut into
quarters

2 large carrots,
unpeeled and
rinsed well,
roughly chopped

1 head garlic,
unpeeled
and rinsed
well, halved
widthwise

4-inch piece fresh
ginger, unpeeled
and rinsed well,
roughly chopped

4-inch piece fresh
turmeric,
unpeeled and
rinsed well,
roughly chopped

*MAKES ABOUT
3 QUARTS*

Tip

*To create an even
fuller, fattier broth,
use an immersion
blender to partially
blend the ingredients
right before straining.*

There's this running joke in my family that my mom is constantly chasing us down with mugs filled with broth screaming, "Drink more soup, it's good for you!" The thing is that it's not really a joke because she is being 100% serious. It doesn't matter what time of the day or night it is; my mom is constantly shoving mugs of broth (always at the perfect drinking temperature) in front of our faces. She genuinely believes her homemade chicken broth is the answer to everything. Did you catch a cold? Drink some broth. Did you lose your job? Drink some broth. Are you gay? Drink as much broth as you can! Well, this is *that broth*. And although it's a labor of love, it's totally worth it. That's not to say it takes a lot of work—just some time to coax the flavors out of the ingredients. What I love about making my own broth is that I use every part of the chicken without wasting a single thing. You get perfectly roasted meat (thanks to my unconventional trick of roasting a whole chicken breast side down, which keeps the white meat moist and juicy while the dark meat finishes cooking), as well as a luxurious elixir from the healthful bones that is extremely flavorful, nourishing, and versatile. You can use the broth in so many different ways, like making soups or braises, or even in place of water to cook rice, but my favorite is simply to sip on it because it's straight-up delicious . . . and, according to my mom, the fix for all life's (supposed) problems.

| Roast the Chicken | Position a rack in the center of the oven and preheat the oven to 400°F. Place the chicken breast side down in a roasting pan. Pat the skin dry with a paper towel. Rub the skin with the oil and season with salt and black pepper. Roast until the thickest part of the chicken reaches 165°F, 65 to 75 minutes. Remove from the oven and let the chicken rest, uncovered, until cool enough to handle, 20 to 30 minutes. Separate the bones and skin from the meat (returning the bones and skin to the roasting pan and storing the meat in an airtight container in the fridge for later use). |

| Make the Broth | In a tall stockpot, add the chicken bones, skin, pan drippings, onion, carrots, garlic, ginger, turmeric, 1 tablespoon salt, and 1 tablespoon black pepper. Cover with enough cold water to fully submerge all the ingredients and bring to a boil. Reduce the heat to a simmer, cover, and cook until the bones and vegetables break down, 2½ to 3 hours, stirring occasionally. |

| Strain the Broth | To strain the broth, ladle the liquid into a fine-mesh sieve (cone shaped is my favorite!) fitted over a large bowl. Do this in batches, discarding the solids as you go. The broth can be used immediately or stored in airtight containers in the fridge for up to 3 days (or in the freezer for up to 6 months). |

Slow-Poached
Soy Sauce
CHICKEN

1½ cups reduced-sodium soy sauce

3 tablespoons granulated sugar

2 tablespoons oyster sauce

1 tablespoon cornstarch

1 tablespoon canola oil

4 cloves garlic, gently crushed

3 scallions, both white and green parts, cut into 2-inch pieces

4-inch piece fresh ginger, thinly sliced

2 bone-in, skin-on chicken breasts (about 2 pounds)

2 bone-in, skin-on chicken leg quarters (about 1½ pounds)

SERVES 4

I love a perfectly roasted chicken as much as the next person, but what if I told you there was another way of preparing everyone's favorite poultry that was equally as delicious and simple? Well, good news, my fellow food lovers, because there is! Say hello to my little friend, the slow-poached soy sauce chicken, also known as "see yao gai" in Cantonese. This chicken is to die for when served warm, but surprisingly, it's just as tasty eaten cold the next day (which is actually a common way of serving it at Chinese restaurants). I'd say that's a win-win if you ask me . . . But wait, there's more! The recipe is super easy (because the stove isn't even on for half the cooking time), fairly forgiving (because instead of a whole chicken it calls for precut, bone-in, skin-on pieces), and yields super-moist, full-flavored meat (thanks to the delicate aromatics and not-too-salty stewed soy sauce). Lastly, if you prefer a certain cut of chicken (white versus dark), feel free to make this using all of one or the other.

| Prepare the Poaching Liquid | In a medium bowl, whisk together the soy sauce, sugar, oyster sauce, and cornstarch until the sugar dissolves. In a large pot (with a tight-fitting lid) over medium heat, add the oil, garlic, scallions, and ginger and cook until the scallions have softened, 3 to 4 minutes, stirring occasionally. Whisk in the soy sauce mixture. |

| Poach the Chicken | Place the chicken pieces skin side down in a single layer into the poaching liquid. Add just enough water to cover and bring to a boil. Immediately reduce the heat to the lowest setting, cover, and cook, undisturbed, for 20 minutes. Without removing the lid, turn the heat off and let the chicken continue to cook (still covered) in the residual heat until the thickest piece of chicken registers 165°F, 25 to 30 minutes. Using tongs, transfer the chicken pieces to a cutting board and let rest for 10 to 15 minutes, making sure to reserve the poaching liquid. Carve the chicken pieces (or not, it's up to you) and serve with a side of poaching liquid. |

BUTTER CHICKEN *Meatballs*

¼ cup panko
    breadcrumbs

¼ cup grated
    Parmesan
    cheese

¼ cup mayonnaise

½ teaspoon garlic
    powder

½ teaspoon onion
    powder

Kosher salt

Freshly ground black
    pepper

1 large egg

1 pound ground
    chicken

6 tablespoons
    (¾ stick)
    unsalted butter

½ medium onion,
    chopped

2 teaspoons garam
    masala

2 teaspoons ground
    turmeric

2 teaspoons grated
    fresh ginger

4 cloves garlic,
    minced

¼ cup tomato paste

1¼ cups chicken
    stock

¾ cup heavy cream

Fresh cilantro,
    roughly
    chopped, for
    garnish

3 cups cooked long-
    grain rice, for
    serving

Naan bread, warmed,
    for serving

SERVES 4

Some say the key to a happy marriage is communication, but I say it's big, juicy balls. Whether they're made of pork, beef, or chicken, they must be big and juicy. All I know is that Doug and I have never been mad at each other while eating meatballs. In fact, our mutual love of the almighty meatball has truly stood the test of time. In this particular recipe, the meatball mix is kind of sticky, but that's how you get really tender, moist meatballs that simultaneously absorb and enhance the flavor of the full-bodied sauce—a creamy, buttery, tomato gravy perfectly seasoned with fragrant garam masala. And since the meatballs are baked (and not seared) before being simmered in the sauce, they require minimal babysitting. In fact, I suggest doubling this recipe since both the sauce and meatballs freeze beautifully (just make sure you freeze them separately).

Make the Meatballs

Position a rack in the center of the oven and preheat the oven to 375°F. Line a large rimmed baking sheet with parchment paper and set aside. In a large bowl, whisk together the panko, Parmesan, mayonnaise, garlic powder, onion powder, ¼ teaspoon salt, ¼ teaspoon black pepper, and the egg until combined. Add the ground chicken and mix until just combined. Shape the mixture into 1½-inch balls (about 2 tablespoons each, to yield 18 to 20 meatballs) and arrange them on the prepared baking sheet. (If you're using your hands, moisten them with a little bit of water to help prevent the mix from sticking to your fingers.) Bake until lightly browned, 20 to 25 minutes. While the meatballs are in the oven, make the sauce.

Make the Sauce

In a large pot over medium heat, add the butter and onions and season with salt and black pepper. Cook until the onions are translucent and slightly charred on the edges, 8 to 10 minutes, stirring occasionally. Add the garam masala, turmeric, ginger, and garlic and cook until fragrant, 45 to 60 seconds, stirring continuously. Add the tomato paste and stir continuously for 60 seconds. Whisk in the chicken stock and heavy cream and bring to a simmer, scraping the bottom of the pot to loosen any browned bits.

Simmer the Meatballs

When the meatballs are done, add them to the pot and gently roll them around in the sauce until they get evenly coated. Simmer until the sauce has thickened slightly, 6 to 8 minutes. Garnish with cilantro and serve with rice and naan.

Tip

If you don't feel like making the meatballs, simply use bite-size chunks of skinless, boneless dark meat chicken instead.

GARLIC BASIL *Chicken Breast* STIR-FRY ⇒

As most of us have experienced firsthand, chicken breasts are always at risk of being too dry or even chalky at times. Needless to say, the line between raw bird meat and perfectly moist chicken boobies is unforgivingly thin. Thankfully, there's velveting—a simple technique that essentially involves coating pieces of lean protein in cornstarch. Velveting not only tenderizes the chicken but also gives it a silky, out-of-this-world texture while helping the sauce evenly coat the meat. Once the chicken pieces are velveted, my favorite thing to do is make this simple garlic basil chicken stir-fry. Fish sauce and oyster sauce give the dish a flavorful funk, while the scallions and basil make it fragrant and sweet. Say goodbye to dry chicken tits and hello to your new favorite muscle-building comfort food!

CHICKEN

1 pound boneless, skinless chicken breasts, cut into ½-inch-thick strips

2 teaspoons reduced-sodium soy sauce

2 teaspoons cornstarch

SAUCE

2 tablespoons oyster sauce

2 teaspoons fish sauce

2 teaspoons reduced-sodium soy sauce

1 teaspoon granulated sugar

4 cloves garlic, minced

2 tablespoons canola oil, divided

2 scallions, light and dark green parts only, chopped

1 jalapeño pepper, thinly sliced (optional)

1½ cups packed fresh basil leaves (regular or Thai)

2 cups cooked rice, for serving

SERVES 2

| Velvet the Chicken | In a medium bowl, combine the chicken and soy sauce and mix until all the pieces are thoroughly coated. Sprinkle in the cornstarch and mix until the chicken is evenly coated and the cornstarch is absorbed. Let the chicken marinate for 20 to 25 minutes at room temperature, or overnight in the fridge, covered. |

| Make the Sauce | In a small bowl, whisk together the oyster sauce, fish sauce, soy sauce, sugar, garlic, and 3 tablespoons of water until the sugar dissolves. Set aside. |

| Parcook the Chicken | In a large nonstick skillet or wok over medium-high heat, add 1 tablespoon of the oil. When the oil is hot, add the chicken in an even layer and cook, undisturbed, until just browned, 1 to 2 minutes on each side. Don't worry about fully cooking the chicken because it will finish cooking later in the recipe. Transfer the chicken back to the medium bowl and set aside. |

| Stir-Fry the Chicken | In the same large nonstick skillet over medium heat, add the remaining tablespoon of oil. When the oil is hot, add the scallions and jalapeño (if using) and cook until the pepper is tender and slightly charred, 2 to 3 minutes, tossing occasionally. Add the parcooked chicken along with the prepared sauce and toss everything together. Spread the ingredients into an even layer and cook, undisturbed, until the sauce has thickened and the chicken is cooked through, 2 to 3 minutes. |

| Serve | Turn off the heat and add the basil leaves. Gently toss until the basil is slightly wilted. Serve immediately with rice. |

Chicken "Shawarma"

with Garlicky Tahini ✈

Throwing a successful dinner party with friends is not an easy thing to do. First, the host must remain cool, calm, and collected. And second, the food needs to be unfussy, crowd pleasing, and packed with flavor. That's why this sheet-pan chicken "shawarma" is perfect when hosting an intimate, casual dinner gathering. This recipe is my very loose (and low-brow) interpretation of an actual shawarma, which is a popular Middle Eastern dish made by spit roasting multiple layers of sliced meat. Since most of us don't have a spit roast to make authentic shawarma, I find juicy, fatty chicken thighs are the next best thing. Not only can everything be prepared and thrown on a sheet pan ahead of time, but you can even double (or triple) this recipe if need be. After everyone arrives, casually pop the food into the oven, set the timer, and enjoy your company all while dinner practically cooks itself. The only way this could go wrong is if your oven breaks, in which case, just get everyone wasted and order delivery.

CHICKEN "SHAWARMA"

¼ cup plain full-fat Greek yogurt

2 tablespoons fresh lemon juice

2 tablespoons extra virgin olive oil, plus more for drizzling

2 teaspoons ground cumin

1 teaspoon ground cinnamon

1 teaspoon ground turmeric

1 teaspoon smoked paprika

Kosher salt

Freshly ground black pepper

3 cloves garlic, minced

1½ pounds boneless, skinless chicken thighs

1 small red onion, sliced

1 large bell pepper (red, orange, or yellow), seeded and sliced

GARLICKY TAHINI

½ cup tahini

3 tablespoons unseasoned rice vinegar

2 tablespoons fresh lemon juice

1 tablespoon soy sauce

1 teaspoon toasted sesame oil

2 cloves garlic, minced

4 flatbreads (such as flour tortillas or pita bread), warmed

3 Roma tomatoes, sliced

3 Persian cucumbers or ½ English cucumber, sliced

1 lemon, cut into wedges, for serving

SERVES 4

| Prepare the Chicken | Position a rack in the center of the oven and preheat the oven to 450°F. In a large bowl, whisk together the yogurt, lemon juice, olive oil, cumin, cinnamon, turmeric, smoked paprika, ½ teaspoon salt, ½ teaspoon black pepper, and the garlic until combined. Add the chicken thighs and mix until thoroughly coated in the yogurt mixture. Set aside. |

| Roast the Ingredients | On a large rimmed baking sheet, spread the onions and bell pepper in an even layer. Drizzle with olive oil and season with salt and black pepper. Arrange the coated chicken thighs on top of the vegetables and roast until the chicken is cooked through and slightly charred on the edges, 18 to 20 minutes. In the meantime, make the garlicky tahini. |

| Make the Garlicky Tahini | In a small bowl, whisk together the tahini, vinegar, lemon juice, soy sauce, sesame oil, and garlic until smooth, adding water as needed to reach the desired consistency. |

| Serve | Transfer the chicken thighs to a cutting board and slice into ½-inch strips. Top each flatbread with some chicken, onion, bell pepper, tomato, cucumber, and a helping of the garlicky tahini sauce. Serve with a lemon wedge and extra sauce. |

Cozy Chicken &
RICE NOODLE SOUP

4 cups chicken broth, homemade (see page 182) or store-bought

1 cup stemmed and thinly sliced shiitake mushrooms

2 tablespoons fish sauce

1 teaspoon granulated sugar

½ teaspoon five-spice powder

1 large boneless, skinless chicken breast (about ½ pound), room temperature for 30 minutes

6 ounces rice noodles

2 cups packed Tuscan or curly kale leaves, roughly chopped

2 scallions, light and dark green parts only, finely chopped

Toasted sesame oil, for drizzling

Fresh basil leaves, for garnish

1 lime, cut into wedges, for garnish

SERVES 2

People always tell Doug how lucky he is that he married a model turned chef, as if good looks and great food are all that matter in life. Listen, if my husband wants to believe that he sleeps next to a hot snack every night, who am I to tell him otherwise? The truth is, *I'm* the lucky one. Doug is smart, handsome, thoughtful, massages my neck every night, and pretty much does it all—except cook. In our first month dating, I came down with a bad case of strep throat. He immediately took a week off work, flew to LA (he lived in SF at the time), and fed me chicken noodle soup every day until I got better. He kept repeating how bad he felt that the soup was store-bought, but I just couldn't believe this dreamy man was hand feeding me soup! In honor of the moment I knew Doug would be the one I'd be watching trashy reality TV with for the rest of my life, here is the chicken noodle soup that he eventually learned to make for me (despite his lack of cooking abilities) for whenever I'm under the weather . . . or just want a satisfying cozy-ass noodle soup. The broth is reminiscent of Vietnamese pho and filled with nutritious kale, earthy shiitakes, and chewy rice noodles. It's nourishing, satiating, and so easy to throw together that even my culinarily challenged husband can make it.

Cook the Chicken Breast
In a medium pot, combine the broth, mushrooms, fish sauce, sugar, and five-spice powder and bring to a boil. Add the chicken breast to the pot and bring everything back to a boil. Immediately cover with the lid and turn the heat off. Let the chicken poach in the broth until fully cooked, 25 to 30 minutes.

Prepare the Noodles
Prepare the noodles according to the package directions. Drain and divide the noodles into two large soup bowls. Set aside.

Cook the Vegetables
Transfer just the chicken breast to a plate and set aside. Bring the broth to a boil. Add the kale and scallions and cook until the kale is just wilted, 30 to 60 seconds.

Serve
Divide the broth and vegetables into each bowl over the noodles. Shred the chicken breast and divide between the bowls. Drizzle with sesame oil and garnish with fresh basil leaves and lime wedges. Serve immediately.

CRISPY
Chicken Legs
with Creamy Beans & Sausage

2 skin-on, bone-in
  chicken
  legs (about
  1½ pounds)

Kosher salt

Freshly ground black
  pepper

2 tablespoons canola
  oil

1 tablespoon
  unsalted butter

½ medium onion,
  chopped

1 (15.5-ounce)
  can navy or
  cannellini beans,
  rinsed and
  drained

1½ cups sliced
  cooked andouille
  or bratwurst
  sausage

1 cup whole milk or
  half-and-half

½ cup grated
  Parmesan
  cheese

2 cloves garlic,
  minced

Fresh flat-leaf
  parsley, roughly
  chopped, for
  garnish

SERVES 2

I'm not sure if you know this about me, but I'm all about thick thighs and meaty legs. Breasts are nice and all, but big juicy gams are what get me excited. I also happen to really like a good succulent sausage, so it only makes sense that I combine these two things to create the ultimate indulgent comfort food: crispy, juicy, and meaty chicken legs nestled in a chunky stew of fatty sausage and creamy beans. Enough said.

| Brown the Chicken |
Position a rack in the center of the oven and preheat the oven to 425°F. Thoroughly pat dry the chicken legs with a paper towel and season with salt and black pepper. In a large cast-iron skillet over medium heat, add the oil. When the oil is hot, carefully place the chicken legs skin side down into the skillet and cook, undisturbed, until the chicken skin is deep golden brown and crispy, 8 to 10 minutes. Don't cook the other side, since it will finish cooking in the oven. Transfer the chicken legs to a plate, leaving any rendered fat in the skillet.

| Make the Sauce |
Reduce the heat to medium-low and add the butter and onions. Season with salt and black pepper and cook until the onions are translucent and slightly browned, 5 to 6 minutes. Add the beans, sausage, milk, Parmesan, and garlic and bring to a boil, stirring continuously. Remove from the heat.

| Bake the Dish |
Nestle the chicken legs browned side up in the sauce and bake until the thickest part of the chicken registers 165°F, 25 to 30 minutes, depending on the thickness of the chicken legs. Let the chicken rest for about 10 minutes. Garnish with chopped parsley and serve immediately.

CHICKEN

Congee with Pork Floss & XO Sauce

1 tablespoon canola oil

½ pound ground chicken

2 scallions, light and dark green parts only, finely chopped

2 cloves garlic, minced

½ teaspoon ground white pepper

¼ teaspoon kosher salt

¾ cup uncooked short-grain white rice, rinsed and drained

4 cups chicken broth, homemade (see page 182) or store-bought

1 tablespoon reduced-sodium soy sauce

TOPPINGS

Toasted sesame oil, for drizzling

Pork floss, for serving

XO sauce, for serving

2 scallions, dark green parts only, chopped, for garnish

SERVES 4

Growing up as a lanky, awkward Asian kid in a predominantly white Christian school (where everyone knew I was gay and Asian before I even did) was quite stressful on my little soul (thank God for therapy!). After a long day of just trying to fit in and some very confusing jokes and slang terms being tossed my way, few things could comfort me the way this congee did (also known as "jook" in our household). Whenever my mom made it, even the smell could snap me out of an emotional slump. This deeply flavorful and hearty porridge made of ground chicken and rice is like a blank canvas you can dress up with whatever toppings your heart desires. My absolute favorite topping is pork floss (a.k.a. "yuk sung" in Chinese), which is sweet-and-savory dried pork that's been shredded to a cotton candy–like texture (find it online or at your local Asian grocery store). If that's not your thing, you can also top this with shredded cheese, fried eggs, roasted veggies or meats, hot sauce, or maybe even no toppings at all! Whether I've had a rough day or the best day ever, settling into the couch with a big bowl of this congee is just so damn comforting.

Brown the Chicken

In a large pot (with a lid) over medium heat, add the oil. When the oil is hot, add the ground chicken, scallions, garlic, white pepper, and salt and cook until the chicken is browned, 4 to 5 minutes, breaking up any large chunks with a wooden spatula.

Make the Congee

Stir in the rice and cook for 45 seconds, stirring continuously. Add the broth, 4 cups of water, and the soy sauce and bring to a boil. Reduce the heat to a simmer, cover, and cook until the rice grains break down and the congee thickens, about 1 hour, mixing and scraping the bottom of the pot every 20 minutes and adding more water if needed to reach the desired consistency.

Serve

Ladle the congee into serving bowls. Garnish with sesame oil, pork floss, XO sauce, and scallions. Serve immediately.

CARAMEL CHICKEN
with Garlic Coconut Rice

Every relationship has a pretty one and a dependable one. It's obvious that the caramel chicken is the pretty one in this coupling, all shiny, sweet, and seductive, ready to be devoured. However, without the dependable garlic coconut rice, the chicken would be longing for that special something to complement it. Although both the chicken and rice are stars in their own right, the garlic coconut rice quietly steals the show. It may look like plain rice, but when you get a taste of those fragrant, savory grains, your socks are going to blow right off. Luckily, you don't need to choose between the two because both are incredibly easy to make and, like all power couples, even better together.

GARLIC COCONUT RICE

1½ cups uncooked short-grain white rice, rinsed, soaked for 15 minutes, and drained

1 (13.5-ounce) can full-fat coconut milk

6 cloves garlic, minced

CARAMEL CHICKEN

8 bone-in, skin-on chicken thighs (about 3½ pounds)

Kosher salt

Freshly ground black pepper

2 tablespoons canola oil

1 (13.5-ounce) can full-fat coconut milk

2 tablespoons fish sauce

2 tablespoons unseasoned rice vinegar

2 tablespoons fresh orange juice

2 scallions, light and dark green parts only, finely chopped

4 cloves garlic, minced

¼ cup packed light brown sugar

2 scallions, dark green parts only, thinly sliced on the bias, for garnish

1 Fresno chili or jalapeño pepper, thinly sliced, for garnish

SERVES 4

Make the Rice

In a medium pot, combine the rice, coconut milk, 1 cup of water, and garlic and bring to a boil. Reduce the heat to a simmer, cover, and cook for 20 minutes. Turn the heat off and let the rice steam for 10 minutes. Fluff the rice with a fork and cover until needed. (Alternatively, cook the rice in a rice cooker if you have one.) While the rice is cooking, make the chicken.

Sear the Chicken

Thoroughly pat dry the chicken thighs with a paper towel and season with salt and black pepper. In a large cast-iron skillet over medium heat, add the oil. When the oil is hot, add the chicken thighs skin side down and cook, undisturbed, until the skin is deep golden brown, 6 to 7 minutes. There's no need to cook the other side, since they will finish cooking later in the recipe. Turn the heat off and transfer the seared chicken thighs to a plate, leaving any rendered fat in the skillet.

Make the Sauce

In a medium bowl, whisk together the coconut milk, fish sauce, vinegar, orange juice, scallions, and garlic. In the same skillet over medium heat, add the brown sugar and cook until it starts to get slightly darker, 1 to 2 minutes, stirring continuously and scraping the bottom of the skillet with a wooden spatula (make sure to keep an eye on this step or the sugar will burn). Whisk in the coconut milk mixture and bring to a boil.

Finish the Dish

Add the seared chicken thighs skin side down to the sauce and bring to a boil. Reduce the heat to a simmer and cook, uncovered, until the sauce reduces by half, 18 to 20 minutes. Flip the chicken thighs and continue to simmer until the remaining sauce thickens slightly, 10 to 15 more minutes. Divide the garlic coconut rice among four serving dishes and top with the chicken thighs. Garnish with scallions and sliced chilies. Serve immediately.

SPICY

Buttermilk *Fried Chicken*

SANDWICH ➺

CHICKEN

2 boneless, skinless chicken breasts (about 1 pound total)

1 cup buttermilk

1 tablespoon hot sauce (Cholula or sriracha)

1 teaspoon garlic powder

1 teaspoon kosher salt

1 teaspoon freshly ground black pepper

SECRET SAUCE

½ cup mayonnaise

2 teaspoons hot sauce (Cholula or sriracha)

2 teaspoons honey or maple syrup

1 teaspoon smoked paprika

½ teaspoon garlic powder

½ teaspoon onion powder

Cheat day is the one day of the week when I convince myself that my body doesn't absorb calories and allow myself to eat whatever the f*ck I want. And although I generally feel like gobbling up everything under the sun during these glorious twenty-four hours, I almost always end up with a fried chicken sandwich in my mouth at some point. The great thing about making your own fried chicken sandwich is that it's going to be piping hot and exactly the way you like it. Personally, I like the fried chicken part to be crispy and juicy, the secret sauce part to be sweet and spicy, and the bun part to be super soft and buttery. I know everyone has their own opinion on what makes the perfect fried chicken sandwich, so feel free to add whatever kind of condiments or toppings you like. I promise it won't hurt my feelings if you change my recipe, because life is just too short to not eat what you want exactly the way you want it (at least on cheat day).

Flatten the Chicken	Place the chicken breasts in a large freezer bag, squeeze out as much air as possible, and seal. Using the smooth side of a meat mallet, gently pound the chicken breasts until they are about ½ inch thick. Remove them from the bag and cut in half widthwise.
Marinate the Chicken	In a small bowl, whisk together the buttermilk, hot sauce, garlic powder, salt, and black pepper until combined and pour into a large freezer bag (use a new one just in case you created any holes in the previous bag). Add the chicken breasts, squeeze out as much air as possible, and seal. Gently massage the marinade into the chicken and refrigerate for at least 4 hours, or overnight.
Make the Sauce	In a small bowl, whisk together the mayonnaise, hot sauce, honey, smoked paprika, garlic powder, and onion powder until combined. Cover with plastic wrap and transfer to the fridge until needed.

Canola oil, for frying

BREADING

1 cup all-purpose
flour

¼ cup cornstarch

1 teaspoon onion
powder

1 teaspoon garlic
powder

1 teaspoon smoked
paprika

1 teaspoon kosher
salt

1 teaspoon freshly
ground black
pepper

4 tablespoons
mayonnaise

4 medium brioche
buns, King's
Hawaiian sweet
bread, or potato
buns

Pickle slices or
kimchi, for
serving

SERVES 4

Fry the Chicken

Preheat the oven to 200°F. Line a large rimmed baking sheet with an oven-safe wire rack and set aside. In a large Dutch oven (or pot with a heavy bottom) over medium heat, add 1½ to 2 inches of oil. Heat the oil to 350°F, adjusting the heat level as needed. (If you don't have a candy thermometer to measure the oil temperature, stick a wooden spoon into the hot oil, and if the oil fizzes gently, then it's ready for the chicken!) In a shallow dish, whisk together the flour, cornstarch, onion powder, garlic powder, smoked paprika, salt, and black pepper. Working in batches, remove the chicken from the marinade and dredge each piece in the flour mixture until thoroughly coated, making sure to firmly press the flour mixture into every nook and cranny. Without overcrowding the pot, slide the floured chicken into the hot oil and fry until golden brown and the internal temperature reaches 165°F, 3 to 5 minutes on each side, depending on the thickness of each piece. Transfer the fried chicken to the wire rack–lined baking sheet and keep warm in the oven while you cook the rest of the chicken.

Assemble the Sandwich

Spread ½ tablespoon of mayonnaise on each cut side of the buns. In a large nonstick skillet over medium-low heat, toast the buns cut side down until golden brown, 1 to 2 minutes. To assemble each sandwich, spread a couple tablespoons of secret sauce on the bottom bun, followed by the pickles, fried chicken breast, and top bun. Serve immediately.

Tip

Always store raw meat on the lowest level in your fridge. That way, if there's any sort of leakage, it doesn't drip onto anything else.

ORANGE *Spatchcock* CHICKEN

Orange chicken smooshes two of my favorite foods (oranges and chicken) into one sweet and tantalizing dish. Unfortunately, I often find the takeout version super disappointing, with chicken scraps covered in a too-thick layer of deep-fried breading. Would it be so hard to use chicken pieces larger than a jelly bean?! I'm not going to call anyone out here, but I've been hurt far too many times by untrustworthy orange chicken. Now that I've said that out loud, I can finally move on emotionally . . . and introduce you to my own version of this iconic takeout dish—a perfectly roasted *whole* chicken smothered in a sweet-and-spicy orange sauce made with *real* oranges. I like to spatchcock my chicken, which results in faster, more even cooking and crispier skin. Spatchcocking a whole chicken isn't as scary as it sounds. I explain exactly how to do it in this recipe, but if you're intimidated, feel free to have your butcher do it for you. Ever since I started making this recipe, I've stopped ordering the takeout version because I've learned that I don't need someone else's orange chicken to make me happy.

1 whole chicken
    (3½ to
    4½ pounds)

2 tablespoons
    unsalted butter,
    softened

Kosher salt

Freshly ground black
    pepper

½ cup freshly
    squeezed
    orange juice

3 tablespoons honey

2 tablespoons
    unsalted butter

2 tablespoons hot
    sauce (Cholula
    or sriracha
    works great!)

1 teaspoon crushed
    red pepper
    flakes

2 cloves garlic,
    minced

1 small orange, cut
    into wedges, for
    serving

SERVES 4

Spatchcock the Chicken

Place the whole chicken breast side down with the neck facing away from you on a baking sheet (or cutting board). Using meat shears or a very sharp knife, cut along each side of the backbone, starting from the rear all the way up to the neck and cutting through the rib bones (much easier than it sounds), until the backbone is removed. Flip the chicken breast side up and tuck the wings under the breasts. Using your palms, firmly press down on the breastbone until you hear a crack (yes, kind of brutal sounding) to flatten the chicken. Congrats! You have successfully spatchcocked a whole chicken!

Roast the Chicken

Position a rack in the center of the oven and preheat the oven to 400°F. Line a large rimmed baking sheet with parchment paper. Place the spatchcocked chicken skin side up on the prepared baking sheet and thoroughly pat dry with a paper towel. Let the chicken come to room temperature, about 30 minutes. Rub the butter all over the chicken skin and season with salt and black pepper. Roast until deep golden brown and the thickest part of the chicken registers 165°F, 50 to 65 minutes, depending on the size of your chicken. Let the chicken rest, uncovered, at room temperature for 15 to 20 minutes while you make the sauce.

Make the Sauce

In a small saucepan over medium-high heat, whisk together the orange juice, honey, butter, hot sauce, pepper flakes, and garlic and cook until the mixture bubbles aggressively and reduces by half, 4 to 5 minutes, whisking often. Using a pastry brush, smother the chicken with the sauce and serve warm with orange wedges on the side.

How to Spatchcock a Chicken

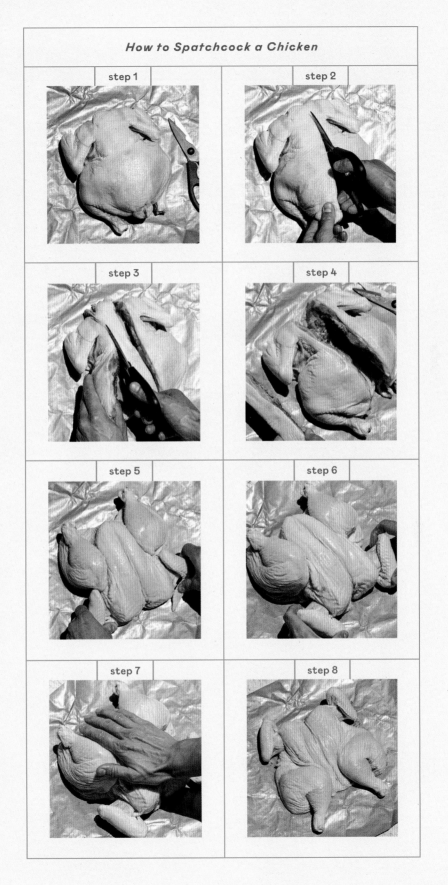

step 1

step 2

step 3

step 4

step 5

step 6

step 7

step 8

For the Love of Seafood

Chili Garlic
SHRIMP

I don't know what it is, but everybody goes gaga over shrimp. I once described them to my mother-in-law as, "sh*t-eating insects of the ocean," and it grossed her out so much she straight up stopped eating shrimp. Then a week later she couldn't help herself and started eating them again. Behold, the power of shrimp! This recipe is for people who unabashedly *love* shrimp and sucking the hepatopancreas (I googled that word) out of their heads. I admit that word isn't the most appetizing, but, trust me, that midgut gland is a one-way ticket to flavor town! Spicy, garlicky, buttery shrimp with a touch of hepatopancreas—what more could you ask for? And if you aren't into sucking on tasty-ass shrimp head innards, pass them over and I'll happily suck them for you.

6 tablespoons (¾ stick) unsalted butter

1 pound extra-large shell-on shrimp (preferably head-on)

4 jalapeño peppers and/or Fresno chilies, sliced, seeds optional

1 tablespoon reduced-sodium soy sauce

6 cloves garlic, minced

1 small navel or blood orange, cut into wedges, for serving

Crusty bread, for serving

SERVES 2

Tip

When buying whole shrimp, try to find the ones that are still swimming in a live tank (you might have to venture to your local fishmonger or Asian grocery store, but I promise you it's worth it). And if you can't locate whole shrimp, look for the headless, shell-on kind (you'll miss out on those succulent shrimp heads, but at least you'll still get that extra layer of flavor from the shells).

Cook the Shrimp

In a large skillet or wok over medium heat, melt the butter. When the butter has melted, add the shrimp and cook until the shells are lightly browned, 2 to 3 minutes on each side. Add the jalapeños and cook until the shrimp turn opaque and curl up, 1 to 2 more minutes, tossing continuously. Add the soy sauce and garlic and cook until fragrant, 30 to 45 seconds, tossing continuously.

Serve

Transfer to a serving dish with orange wedges and crusty bread. Serve immediately.

AHI TUNA & SALMON

Poke Bowls
with Brown Sushi Rice

QUICK-PICKLED RADISHES

2 tablespoons unseasoned rice vinegar

1 teaspoon granulated sugar

½ teaspoon kosher salt

4 radishes, halved and thinly sliced into half moons

BROWN SUSHI RICE

¾ cup uncooked brown short-grain rice, rinsed and drained

2 tablespoons unseasoned rice vinegar

2 teaspoons granulated sugar

½ teaspoon kosher salt

SALMON & TUNA POKE

2 tablespoons reduced-sodium soy sauce

1 tablespoon fresh lemon juice

1 tablespoon toasted sesame oil

2 teaspoons toasted sesame seeds

10 ounces skinless sushi-grade ahi tuna and/or salmon, cut into ½-inch cubes

1 avocado, cut into 8 wedges

Tobiko (flying fish roe), for garnish (optional)

Quick Spicy Mayo (page 37), for serving

Lemon wedges, for garnish

SERVES 2

It doesn't matter whether you've never cooked a single piece of fish in your life or you happen to be Fish Cooker McFisherman because this recipe doesn't require any cooking at all! Back in the day, native Hawaiian fishermen would slice off little pieces of raw fish from their daily catch, season them, and eat them as a snack—this is what we now know as poke. As the years went by and Japanese influence became more prominent in Hawaii, poke bowls began to appear—the beautiful and tasty love child of poke and donburi (a Japanese rice bowl). A true Hawaiian poke bowl has only a few toppings—allowing the flavor of the fish to really shine, which is why the most important component of a kick-ass poke bowl comes down to using the freshest sushi-grade fish you can find. The combination of chewy brown rice, crunchy and vinegary radishes, and creamy avocado alongside lightly seasoned fish and tobiko makes for a delightfully satisfying and Instagrammable bowl of grub.

Pickle the Radishes

In a shallow medium bowl, whisk together the vinegar, sugar, and salt until the sugar dissolves. Add the radishes and toss to combine. Transfer to the fridge until needed.

Make the Rice

In a small saucepan (with a lid), combine the brown rice and 1½ cups of water and bring to a boil. Reduce the heat to a simmer, cover, and cook until the water is absorbed and the rice is tender, 35 to 40 minutes. Turn the heat off and let steam, covered, for 10 minutes. While the rice is still hot, mix in the vinegar, sugar, and salt until thoroughly combined. The mixture may look kind of wet, but cover it again, and it will be ready to go by the time you assemble the bowls.

Make the Poke

In a medium bowl, whisk together the soy sauce, lemon juice, sesame oil, and sesame seeds until combined. Add the fish and gently toss to coat.

Assemble the Bowls

Divide the rice between two serving bowls and top with the seasoned fish, pickled radishes, avocado, and some tobiko (if using). Serve with the Quick Spicy Mayo and lemon wedges on the side.

Broiled
BRANZINO
with Citrus Ponzu Sauce

1 whole branzino,
    Thai snapper, or
    pompano (about
    1¼ pounds),
    scaled, gutted,
    and trimmed

1 tablespoon canola
    oil

Kosher salt

Freshly ground black
    pepper

4 cloves garlic,
    crushed

1 medium navel or
    blood orange,
    half squeezed,
    half sliced

1 lemon, half
    squeezed, half
    sliced

1 lime, half squeezed,
    half sliced

2 teaspoons
    reduced-sodium
    soy sauce

½ teaspoon
    granulated
    sugar

Fresh cilantro
    leaves, for
    garnish

SERVES 2

A lot of people don't know this about me, but I'm a bona fide fisherman and the Little Mermaid is my spirit animal (even if she does have a very serious hoarding problem). You can't tell just by looking at my goofy mug, but I have a deep understanding and passion for all things fishing. I know the different methods of catching fish and what's needed to hook various species. I know the give and take of reeling in a fighter and the sheer excitement of finding out what you caught. And once a fish is in the boat, I can scale, gut, and trim that sucker with my eyes closed. Most important, I know the best way to cook fish—which is quick and simple. If an entire fish can fit on a baking sheet, it should be broiled whole (or grilled!). Much like roasting a whole chicken, the skin and bones help keep the meat moist and flavorful; plus it's just a beautifully lazy way of making delicious fish. To finish it off, I like to drizzle the fish with my sweet-and-tangy citrus ponzu, which not only highlights the freshness of the fish but pairs perfectly with the slight char resulting from the high-heat cooking. When it comes to the type of fish to buy for this recipe, branzino tends to be the easiest to find, but any other whole medium-size fish, such as Thai snapper, porgy, or pompano, will work just as marvelously.

| Prep the Fish | Position a rack in the center of the broiler and preheat the broiler to high. Place the fish on a large rimmed baking sheet and, using a sharp knife, make three diagonal slits (don't cut through the rib bones) on each side. Rub the oil all over the fish and season with salt and black pepper. Place the garlic cloves and half of the citrus slices into the cavity of the fish. Place the remaining citrus slices underneath the fish and broil until the flesh is flaky and opaque, 12 to 14 minutes. While the fish is cooking, make the citrus ponzu. |

| Make the Citrus Ponzu | In a small bowl, whisk together the freshly squeezed citrus juices, soy sauce, and sugar until the sugar dissolves. |

| Serve | Transfer the entire fish to a serving platter and drizzle half of the citrus ponzu over the fish. Garnish with cilantro and serve immediately with the remaining ponzu on the side. |

Tip

When buying whole fish, look for clear eyes and bright, shiny scales. The fish should smell fresh like the ocean and nothing else. If you aren't comfortable cleaning it yourself, kindly ask your fishmonger to scale, gut, and trim off any spiky fins for you.

Chilean Sea Bass

with Mushroom & Scallion Oil

2 tablespoons yellow
    miso paste

1 tablespoon
    unseasoned rice
    vinegar

1 teaspoon packed
    brown sugar
    (light or dark)

2 (6-ounce) fillets
    skinless
    Patagonian
    toothfish (a.k.a.
    Chilean sea
    bass), or any
    other whitefish
    (just adjust the
    roasting time
    accordingly)

**MUSHROOM &
SCALLION OIL**

3 tablespoons extra
    virgin olive oil

2 teaspoons grated
    fresh ginger

2 scallions, dark
    green parts
    only, chopped

1 cup stemmed
    and thinly
    sliced shiitake
    or cremini
    mushrooms

Kosher salt

Freshly ground black
    pepper

2 cups cooked rice,
    for serving

SERVES 2

Hold on to your butts, everyone, because I have a secret to tell you—Chilean sea bass is not a sea bass. It's actually Patagonian toothfish, but since people are weirded out by eating animals with funny names, some clever person at the fish market decided to give it a stage name to make it more palatable to all the basic folks out there. Personally, I think it feels kind of disrespectful to eat something and not even call it by its real name—so from this sentence on I'm calling this fish by its original moniker. Patagonian toothfish happens to be one of my favorite fish in the entire world because its flavor is rich, buttery, and not at all "fishy." The flesh is firm yet flaky and moist. In this recipe, everything from the slightly sweetened miso paste to the flavor-packed mushroom and scallion oil only further highlights the gorgeous flavor and texture of this perfect fish. Every tender bite feels almost sacrilegious, and I'm totally here for it. And because it's so fatty, Patagonian toothfish is virtually impossible to mess up, which makes this the most stress-free seafood you will ever cook.

| Marinate the Fish | Position a rack in the top of the oven and preheat the oven to 425°F. Line a baking sheet with parchment paper. In a small bowl, mix together the miso paste, vinegar, and brown sugar until combined. Pat dry the fish with a paper towel and cover with the miso mixture. Place the fish onto the prepared baking sheet and marinate at room temperature for about 20 minutes. While the fish is marinating, make the oil. |

| Make the Oil | In a small saucepan over medium heat, combine the oil, ginger, scallions, mushrooms, salt, and black pepper and cook until the mushrooms are half the size, 3 to 4 minutes, stirring occasionally. Turn off the heat and leave on the warm stovetop until needed. |

| Roast the Fish | Roast the fish until flaky and slightly charred on the edges, 14 to 16 minutes. Divide the rice between two serving dishes and top each with a piece of fish. Spoon the warm mushroom and scallion oil on top and serve immediately. |

MUSSEL & CLAM
Soba with Browned
ANCHOVY BUTTER

I'm a lover, not a hater . . . of all types of shellfish, while Doug, on the other hand, only likes mussels. Maybe it has something to do with their slightly different textures or the fact that clams live *in* sand and mussels live *on* rocks, piers, and pilings. Personally, I'm not going to judge how shellfish live their lives, because to me they are equally delicious. However, if you're like Doug and prefer one kind of shellfish over another, feel free to make this recipe with just that one. I don't really feel like I need to sell this umami bomb of a recipe to you, but just in case, you've got mussels and clams tangled up in strands of nutty buckwheat noodles soaking in a briny, garlicky, and ever-so-slightly-spicy broth. Need I say more?

2 pounds fresh littleneck clams, Manila clams, and/or mussels, scrubbed clean

6 ounces dried soba noodles

2 tablespoons unsalted butter

4 anchovy fillets (canned or jarred)

8 cloves garlic, minced

1 tablespoon sambal oelek

½ cup white wine

Kosher salt

Extra virgin olive oil, for drizzling

2 tablespoons finely chopped fresh flat-leaf parsley

Crushed red pepper flakes, for garnish

SERVES 2

Prep the Shellfish

Submerge the clams in very cold water for at least 15 minutes to encourage them to spit out any remaining sand or grit. (If you're using farm-raised clams, feel free to skip this step because most are purged of sand before they hit the market.) For the mussels, pull off any fibrous beards (a.k.a. the byssus thread, which is what the mussel uses to permanently attach itself to things) and rinse the mussels with cold water. Any shellfish that are open and do not close when you tap on them are dead and should be thrown away.

Cook the Soba

Bring a large pot of unsalted water to a rolling boil. Add the soba noodles and cook 1 minute less than al dente according to the package directions. Drain in a colander, rinse with cool water to remove the excess starch, and thoroughly drain again. Divide the soba noodles between two serving bowls and set aside.

Cook the Anchovies

In a large pot (with a tight-fitting lid) over medium heat, add the butter and anchovy fillets and cook until the milk solids in the butter begin to brown and the anchovies soften, 1 to 2 minutes, using a wooden spoon to break them up into teeny-tiny pieces. Stir in the garlic and sambal oelek and cook until fragrant, about 30 seconds.

Cook the Shellfish

Carefully add the shellfish to the pot (so you don't break the shells). Add the wine and a pinch of salt and give everything a gentle stir to combine. Increase the heat to high, cover with the lid, and steam the shellfish until they all open up, 5 to 7 minutes, giving the pot a shake every 2 minutes (without opening the lid). Discard any shellfish that did not open. Divide the shellfish and broth between the two bowls of soba. Garnish with a drizzle of olive oil, chopped parsley, and pepper flakes. Serve immediately.

CRISPY-SKIN

Salmon with Avocado ➤➤ Mango Rice Salad

2 (6-ounce) fillets skin-on salmon, scales removed

2 tablespoons fresh lime juice

2 tablespoons fresh orange juice

2 tablespoons extra virgin olive oil

1 tablespoon toasted sesame oil

2 teaspoons fish sauce

2 cloves garlic, grated

¼ teaspoon kosher salt

1 cup cooked long-grain white rice, cooled

1 cup baby spinach, finely chopped

1 cup cherry tomatoes, quartered

1 cup diced seedless cucumber, such as Persian or English

1 avocado, diced

1 mango, diced

¼ cup slivered almonds

2 tablespoons canola oil

Kosher salt

Fresh cilantro leaves, for garnish

SERVES 2

In my early twenties, I was in a long-distance relationship with a dude who lived in San Francisco, and the very first night he visited me in LA, I offered to cook for him. Ironically, I had never really cooked for anyone before, but I *really* wanted to impress him with my burgeoning culinary skills. Here I was feeling all confident, thinking that I had made the most impressive salmon dish ever—I even made the plating all pretty! As soon as we took a bite, we both spit it out, laughed our tits off, and mutually agreed that it tasted nasty. We named the dish "ASS" and not because of what you might think, but because it was Awfully Sh*tty Salmon! Luckily, my salmon game has improved since then and this crispy-skin salmon recipe has become my go-to. The secret to super-crispy skin is to remove the scales, "air dry" the salmon in the fridge, and start with a room-temperature skillet. As the skillet heats, the skin will get shatteringly crispy while the flesh cooks to the perfect temperature. Then I pair the fish with a refreshing, colorful rice salad filled with creamy avocado, sweet mango, and crunchy cucumbers. If I've learned anything from that night of ASS, it's that you should never be afraid to experiment in the kitchen, even if it's for a first date. If all goes well, somebody is going to be impressed, and if it doesn't, you might just find the love of your life.

| Prep the Salmon | Thoroughly pat dry the salmon fillets with a paper towel and place them on a cutting board. If you have fillets with scales still on, use the sharp edge of a knife to remove the scales by carefully scraping them off in the opposite direction to how they lie on the fish with short back-and-forth motions. Brush off any loose scales and place the salmon skin side up on a paper towel–lined plate. Transfer to the fridge, uncovered, and refrigerate for at least 30 minutes (or overnight) to allow the excess moisture to evaporate from the skin. Meanwhile, make the vinaigrette and rice salad. |

| Make the Vinaigrette | In a small bowl, whisk together the lime juice, orange juice, olive oil, sesame oil, fish sauce, garlic, and salt until combined. Set aside. |

| Make the Rice Salad | In a large bowl, combine the rice, spinach, tomatoes, cucumbers, avocado, mango, almonds, and one-quarter of the vinaigrette and toss to combine, adding more vinaigrette as needed. Reserve the remaining vinaigrette for serving. Divide the rice salad between two serving dishes and set aside. |

Cook the Salmon

In a room-temperature medium nonstick skillet, add the canola oil and swirl it around so it evenly coats the bottom. Season both sides of the chilled salmon fillets with salt and place them skin side down a couple of inches apart in the skillet. Set the skillet over medium heat and use a large spatula to firmly press down on the salmon, which will keep the skin flat on the hot surface to help it get super crispy. Do this for the first 3 to 4 minutes, then release the spatula and let the fish cook, undisturbed, until the sides are opaque and light pink, 2 to 4 more minutes, depending on the thickness of your fillets. Turn the heat off, flip the salmon, and let the residual heat cook the fish for 1 to 2 more minutes. Top the rice salad with the salmon (crispy skin side up!) and garnish with cilantro before serving.

Tip

The best way to tell if a mango is ripe is to SMELL IT!!! If the fruit smells like it would taste delicious, then it most likely will. Before adding the mango to the rest of the ingredients, give it a quick taste to make sure you like the flavor and texture. If you don't, you should just toss it because a bad mango will ruin this dish (and your life)!

Scallops with Corn & Coconut Broth

8 to 10 large scallops

1 tablespoon yellow miso paste

2 tablespoons extra virgin olive oil, plus more for drizzling

1½ cups sweet corn kernels (from about 3 ears), preferably fresh, but canned or frozen works too

4 scallions, light and dark green parts only, finely chopped

1 teaspoon grated fresh ginger

2 cloves garlic, minced

½ teaspoon kosher salt

1 cup full-fat coconut milk

¼ cup canola oil

Kosher salt

Freshly ground black pepper

Fresh basil leaves, for garnish

Fresh cilantro leaves, for garnish

SERVES 2

Tip

If you are working with frozen scallops, make sure they are completely thawed in the fridge before starting this recipe. Otherwise, liquid will leak out when you cook them and the scallops will steam instead of sear.

My mom is a three-star Yelp review come to life. Nothing she eats is ever really all *that* good, and she never hesitates to tell you what she would have done differently had she cooked it. The thing is, I love it when people enjoy my cooking because getting validation is fun—that's why cooking for my mom can be somewhat intimidating. Fortunately, whenever I need to impress even the harshest critics, these pan-seared scallops snuggled in a warm corn and coconut broth never disappoint (unless the critic has a shellfish allergy). In fact, this happens to be one of Mama Woo's favorite dishes that I make (so you know it must be good)! The headliner of this recipe might be the scallops, but the real scene-stealer is the surprisingly quick broth that sits underneath those suckers. It feels like a light miso coconut chowder that's chock-full of crunchy corn and aromatics. So even if you don't cook the scallops perfectly, I promise no one will even notice because the broth is just that damn good.

Prep the Scallops	Thoroughly pat dry the scallops with a paper towel and place on a paper towel–lined plate. Transfer to the fridge, uncovered, and refrigerate for at least 15 to 20 minutes (or overnight) to allow excess moisture to evaporate from their surface.
Make the Broth	In a small bowl, whisk together the miso paste and ½ cup of water until smooth. In a medium saucepan over medium-high heat, combine the olive oil, corn, scallions, ginger, garlic, and salt and cook until fragrant, 2 to 3 minutes, stirring often. Add the coconut milk and miso water and bring to a boil. Cook until the broth is reduced by half, 5 to 6 minutes, stirring occasionally. While the broth is cooking, sear the scallops.
Sear the Scallops	In a large cast-iron skillet over medium-high heat, add the canola oil. While the oil is heating up, remove the scallops from the fridge and season both sides with salt and black pepper (do this right before cooking; otherwise the salt will draw out more moisture!). When the oil is hot, carefully arrange the scallops about 1 inch apart in the skillet and cook, undisturbed, until deep golden brown, 3 to 4 minutes. (Don't be tempted to check on them until at least the 3-minute mark.) Using tongs, flip the scallops and cook the other side until golden brown, 2 to 3 minutes, keeping in mind that this side won't get as brown. Immediately transfer the scallops to a plate.
Serve	Divide the corn and coconut broth between two serving dishes and top with the seared scallops. Garnish with a drizzle of olive oil and basil and cilantro leaves. Serve immediately.

Bring Out the Meat

Pan-Seared *Fish Sauce* PORK CHOPS

4 bone-in pork rib chops or loin chops (about 3 pounds), 1 inch thick

2 tablespoons fish sauce

2 tablespoons unseasoned rice vinegar

2 tablespoons honey

2 tablespoons ketchup

2 tablespoons canola oil

Kosher salt

Freshly ground black pepper

2 tablespoons unsalted butter

SERVES 4

Although the name of this cookbook is inspired by my mom, my dad deserves just as much credit for my intense love of food. While Mama Woo is a pro at making delicious grub, Papa Woo is a pro at enjoying it. Sometimes, I think he loves food more than he loves his own kids, but I don't blame him since food won't drop out of college, move to LA to become a model, and then later tell you they're gay. (For the record, I did make a living as a working model, go back to college, and ultimately graduate with two master's degrees.) All that might have been enough to melt the brain of a self-made immigrant like my father, but he eventually came around. It took a few years, but I remember the exact moment he did. It was during one of his visits to LA, and I had just prepared his absolute favorite thing in all the land—pan-seared thick-cut pork chops. I knew he was hungry, but as he was about to dig into his pork chop he turned to me and said that all he ever wanted was for me to be happy and that he was proud of me for always following my own path no matter what. Then he dove right into that pork chop, and the rest is history. I'm not saying these perfectly caramelized, juicy, and umami-packed (thanks, fish sauce!) pork chops were the catalyst for my father's reassuring words, but the man sure does love to eat—and good food can be truly life changing.

Prep the Sauce

Thoroughly pat dry the pork chops with a paper towel and let them come to room temperature, 20 to 30 minutes. In a small bowl, whisk together the fish sauce, vinegar, honey, and ketchup. Set aside.

Cook the Pork Chops

Rub the oil on both sides of the pork chops and season with salt and black pepper. Heat a large cast-iron skillet over medium-high heat. When the skillet is hot, add the pork chops and cook, undisturbed, until deep golden brown and slightly charred on the edges, 5 to 7 minutes on each side. Transfer to a serving plate and let rest for 10 to 15 minutes while you make the sauce.

Make the Sauce

In a small saucepan over medium heat, add the butter and the fish sauce mixture and cook until slightly thickened, 2 to 3 minutes, whisking continuously. Spoon the warm sauce over the pork chops and serve immediately.

Gochujang Grilled
SKIRT STEAK

2 tablespoons
  gochujang

2 tablespoons
  mayonnaise

1 tablespoon
  reduced-sodium
  soy sauce

2 teaspoons packed
  brown sugar
  (light or dark)

2 teaspoons toasted
  sesame seeds,
  plus more for
  garnish

1 teaspoon toasted
  sesame oil

4 cloves garlic,
  minced

2 scallions, light
  and dark green
  parts only, thinly
  sliced, reserve
  1 teaspoon for
  garnish

1½ pounds skirt
  steak (flank
  steak, hangar
  steak, or flap
  meat works too),
  trimmed

SERVES 4

I rarely ever judge people, but when I do it's because of how they like their steak. If a person enjoys their steak rare, they're either adventurous or old. If someone prefers their steak medium-rare, they're good people and I just know we'll be best friends forever. And if a person says they like their steak well-done, they're either kidding around or a total psychopath. Luckily for these questionable individuals, there's skirt steak, which is super forgiving and always turns out tasty no matter the preferred level of doneness. The marinade here is sweet, salty, and a little spicy (thanks to the gochujang) and really complements the smokiness from grilling the steak. And if you don't feel like turning on the barbecue, you can broil the steak, which is a great way to replicate some of that smoky char you get from grilling.

| Marinate the Steak | In a small bowl, mix together the gochujang, mayonnaise, soy sauce, brown sugar, sesame seeds, sesame oil, garlic, and scallions until combined. Scrape the mixture into a large freezer bag. Add the skirt steak, squeeze out as much air as possible, and seal. Massage the marinade into the steak and refrigerate for at least 4 hours, or overnight. |

| Cook the Steak | Preheat your grill to high heat. Remove the steak from the marinade and, using a paper towel, wipe off excess marinade. Discard the leftover marinade. Cook the steak on the hot grill for 2 to 5 minutes on each side, depending on your preferred level of doneness. Transfer the steak to a cutting board and let rest for 15 minutes. Thinly slice against the grain and garnish with toasted sesame seeds and scallions before serving. |

Firecracker
GAME HENS

¼ cup unseasoned
rice vinegar

¼ cup canola oil,
plus more for
shallow-frying

2 tablespoons
smoked paprika

2 tablespoons finely
chopped fresh
flat-leaf parsley

1 tablespoon sambal
oelek, plus more
for serving

1 teaspoon kosher
salt

1 teaspoon freshly
ground black
pepper

4 cloves garlic,
minced

2 Cornish game
hens, backbone
removed and
halved

1 lime, cut into
wedges, for
serving

SERVES 2

I'm oddly drawn to things that are either absurdly ginormous or super tiny (for example, my dogs!), which is probably what led me to these adorable little Cornish game hens in the first place. Just look at them—they're almost too cute to eat (don't worry, I said *almost*)! They have just the right amount of both white and dark meat, making each bird a perfectly sized individual serving (unless you're a 6'2", 185-pound human garbage disposal like me, in which case I usually eat two). You might be wondering why not just roast a whole chicken instead? First, Cornish game hens are easier to handle and cook faster than other poultry due to their size. Second, these little guys are experts at soaking up marinade because there's less meat to penetrate, making each bite juicy and incredibly flavorful. Speaking of, the kick-ass marinade in this recipe gives you smoky, spicy, tangy vibes (not to mention gorgeous color), and the moment it hits your tongue will explode with flavor (hence the name "firecracker").

| Marinate the Game Hens | In a small bowl, whisk together the vinegar, oil, smoked paprika, parsley, sambal oelek, salt, black pepper, and garlic until combined. Transfer the marinade to a large freezer bag. Add the Cornish game hens, squeeze out as much air as possible, and seal. Gently massage the marinade into the game hens and refrigerate for at least 4 hours, or overnight. |

| Sear the Game Hens | Position a rack in the center of the oven and preheat the oven to 375°F. Line a plate with two layers of paper towels. Remove the game hens from the marinade and transfer to the paper towel–lined plate. Discard any leftover marinade. Pat dry the skin with another paper towel and let them come to room temperature, 20 to 30 minutes. In a large cast-iron skillet over medium heat, add ¼ inch of canola oil. When the oil is hot, carefully place the game hens skin side down in the skillet and cook, undisturbed, until the skin is golden brown and crispy, 3 to 4 minutes. |

| Roast the Game Hens | Transfer the game hens to a baking sheet skin side up and roast until cooked through, 18 to 22 minutes, depending on the size of the hens. Let the hens rest for 10 to 15 minutes. Serve with lime wedges and more sambal oelek. |

BULGOGI

Pork Tenderloin
Lettuce Wraps

2 tablespoons reduced-sodium soy sauce

1 tablespoon toasted sesame oil

1 teaspoon packed brown sugar (light or dark)

½ teaspoon freshly ground black pepper

3 scallions, light and dark green parts only, finely chopped

3 cloves garlic, minced

1 pound pork tenderloin, sliced into ½-inch thick rounds

2 tablespoons canola oil

2 cups cooked short-grain rice (white or brown)

1½ cups shredded mozzarella

Toasted sesame seeds, for garnish

12 iceberg lettuce or butter lettuce leaves, for serving

Bibimbap-Style Sauce (page 35), for serving

SERVES 4

The best thing about being in a loving, committed relationship is having the freedom to eat dinner like a barbarian with your bare hands whenever you feel like it. If it's a *really* special occasion, I'll put on a pair of latex gloves like a sexy surgeon and go to town on my food like one of those people in an ASMR video on YouTube. Doug doesn't even bat an eye as I'm casually shoveling food into my mouth using all ten fingers—that's true love, folks. So, if you're anything like me and have a thing for extremely tasty food meant to be eaten with your hands, these meaty pork lettuce wraps are for you. The tender charred pork tenderloin, cheesy rice, crunchy lettuce, and spicy bibimbap-style sauce all work together to create "finger food" magic. No forks and knives allowed tonight!

Cook the Pork

In a medium bowl, whisk together the soy sauce, sesame oil, brown sugar, black pepper, scallions, and garlic until the sugar dissolves. Add the sliced pork and toss until thoroughly coated in the mixture. Heat a large cast-iron skillet over medium-high heat. When the skillet is hot, arrange the pork in an even layer and cook, undisturbed, until slightly charred, 2 to 3 minutes on each side. (Alternatively, the pork slices can be skewered and grilled.) Transfer the cooked pork to a plate and set aside.

Crisp Up the Rice

In a large nonstick skillet over medium heat, add the canola oil and rice and toss to combine. Spread the rice into an even layer and cook, undisturbed, until the bottom of the rice is crispy, 5 to 7 minutes. Sprinkle the shredded mozzarella on top and continue cooking, undisturbed, until the cheese has melted, 2 to 3 minutes. Top with the cooked pork and garnish with toasted sesame seeds. Serve family style with the lettuce and bibimbap-style sauce.

Sweet & Sticky LAMB RIB CHOP "Satay"

½ cup full-fat coconut milk

4 teaspoons reduced-sodium soy sauce, divided

1 teaspoon fish sauce

1 teaspoon curry powder

1 teaspoon grated fresh ginger

1 (8-rib) rack of lamb (about 1¼ pounds), trimmed and cut into double chops

2 tablespoons honey

2 cloves garlic, minced

Fresh cilantro, roughly chopped, for garnish

SERVES 2

Lamb rib chops cook up incredibly quickly and are really hard to mess up. On top of that, these adorable meat morsels come with their own little handle—almost like they are just begging to be eaten! Although this isn't your typical satay recipe, I promise all those delicious flavors you expect from a mouthwatering satay are here . . . only better. The marinade is a little sweet, a little funky, and deeply flavorful—it can also be used to marinate chicken drumsticks, beef skewers, or even shrimp. If you're on the fence about lamb, this is the perfect gateway recipe. And if you already love lamb, I guarantee this will make you love it even more.

Make the Marinade

In a small bowl, whisk together the coconut milk, 2 teaspoons of the soy sauce, the fish sauce, curry powder, and ginger until combined. Pour the marinade into a large freezer bag. Add the lamb rib chops, squeeze out as much air as possible, and seal. Massage the marinade into the lamb and refrigerate for at least 4 hours, or overnight.

Cook the Lamb

Position a rack in the center of the oven and preheat the oven to 375°F. Line a plate with two layers of paper towels. Remove the lamb rib chops from the marinade and transfer to the paper towel–lined plate. Using another paper towel, wipe off any excess marinade from the lamb rib chops and discard the leftover marinade. Heat a large cast-iron skillet over medium-high heat. When the skillet is hot, add the lamb rib chops (about 1 inch apart) and cook, undisturbed, until deep golden brown and slightly charred, 2 to 3 minutes. Flip the lamb rib chops and transfer the entire skillet to the oven. Roast until the lamb rib chops are medium-rare, 6 to 7 minutes (add 1 to 2 more minutes for medium doneness). Let the lamb rib chops rest in the skillet, uncovered, at room temperature for 10 minutes while you make the sauce.

Make the Sauce

In a small saucepan over medium heat, combine the honey, the remaining 2 teaspoons of soy sauce, and the garlic. Cook until fragrant and the mixture begins to bubble, about 1 minute, stirring continuously. Drizzle the sauce over the lamb rib chops. Garnish with the cilantro and serve immediately.

Perfect GARLIC BUTTER RIB EYE
with Crunchy Ginger Rice

1½-inch-thick
bone-in rib eye
steak (about
1½ pounds)

1½ cups cooked rice
(long or short
grain)

1 tablespoon grated
fresh ginger

1 teaspoon reduced-
sodium soy
sauce

1 tablespoon canola
oil

Kosher salt

Freshly ground black
pepper

4 tablespoons
(½ stick)
unsalted butter

4 cloves garlic,
minced

SERVES 2

To this day, rib eye steak is still my favorite cut of meat, although now it's more of a treat as opposed to a twice-weekly dinner. That's why when I do crave it, the rib eye has to be spot-on. I want a juicy, well-marbled, and flavorful steak smothered in butter and garlic and cooked to medium-rare perfection. And since I'm already going there, how about some ultra-flavorful crunchy ginger rice? Because all that delicious garlic butter left in the skillet is used to crisp up this sweet, aromatic rice, everything also happens to be cooked in the same pan. Sounds pretty damn perfect to me.

Prep the Rice

Thoroughly pat dry the steak with a paper towel and let it come to room temperature, about 30 minutes. In a medium bowl, mix together the cooked rice, ginger, and soy sauce until combined. Set aside.

Cook the Steak

Rub the oil on both sides of the steak and season with salt and black pepper. Heat a large cast-iron skillet over medium-high heat. When the skillet is hot, add the steak and, using a spatula, press it into the skillet (to maximize surface contact) for about 30 seconds. Continue cooking the steak, undisturbed, until deep golden brown and slightly charred, 4 to 6 minutes on each side. Turn the heat off.

Baste the Steak

Immediately add the butter and garlic to the hot skillet. Continuously spoon the melting garlic butter all over the steak for 1 minute. Transfer the steak to a cutting board and let rest, uncovered, for 10 to 15 minutes. Carefully pour all the melted butter from the skillet into a small bowl and set aside.

Cook the Rice

In the same skillet over medium heat, add 1 tablespoon of the reserved garlic butter along with the ginger rice mixture and toss to combine, making sure the rice grains are evenly coated in the garlic butter. Spread the rice into an even layer and cook, undisturbed, until lightly browned and crispy, 2 to 3 minutes. Give the rice a quick toss and remove from the heat. Slice the steak and serve with the warm, crunchy ginger rice.

BROILED

Lamb Tacos
with Paprika Lime Sour Cream

MARINATED LAMB

½ cup sour cream or Greek yogurt

2 teaspoons onion powder

2 teaspoons garlic powder

2 teaspoons five-spice powder

1 teaspoon ground cumin

1 teaspoon kosher salt

1 teaspoon freshly ground black pepper

1 pound boneless lamb shoulder, trimmed and untied

PAPRIKA LIME SOUR CREAM

½ cup sour cream or Greek yogurt

1 tablespoon fresh lime juice

1 teaspoon ground smoked paprika

12 mini "street-style" tortillas (corn or flour), warmed

½ cup fresh cilantro (leaves and small stems), hand torn, for serving

1 cup fresh basil, hand torn, for serving

Spicy, Vinegary Shaved Persian Cucumber Salad (page 162), for serving

SERVES 4

On one of our earliest dates, Doug and I decided to get tacos. We went to a hole-in-the-wall with an eclectic menu that had every offering under the sun—including lamb tacos! I love me a good lamb taco and, to my surprise, so did Doug! Could he be the chimi to my changa? The yin to my yang? As I watched my future husband tilt his head to the side and take a bite of that delectable taco looking all sexy and unafraid of eating messy food in front of me, I knew I had found the one. These lamb tacos are my version of *those* lamb tacos. Sappy love story aside, the thinly sliced five-spice-marinated lamb shoulder coupled with spicy-vinegary shaved cucumbers, fresh herbs, and a tangy sour cream drizzle all cuddled inside a warm tortilla make these some of the brightest and tastiest tacos you will ever eat.

Marinate the Lamb

In a small bowl, mix together the sour cream, onion powder, garlic powder, five-spice powder, cumin, salt, and black pepper until combined. Scrape the mixture into a large freezer bag. Add the lamb shoulder, squeeze out as much air as possible, and seal. Massage the marinade into the lamb and refrigerate for at least 4 hours, or overnight.

Make the Paprika Lime Sour Cream

In a small bowl, whisk together the sour cream, lime juice, and smoked paprika until combined. Cover with plastic wrap and refrigerate until needed.

Broil the Lamb

Position a rack in the center of the oven and preheat the broiler to high. Line a large rimmed baking sheet with an oven-safe wire rack. Remove the lamb from the marinade and, using a paper towel, wipe off any excess marinade. Discard the leftover marinade. Place the lamb onto the wire rack–lined baking sheet and let it come to room temperature, about 20 minutes. Broil until golden brown and charred on the edges, 13 to 15 minutes. Transfer to a cutting board and let rest, uncovered, for 15 minutes.

Serve

Thinly slice the lamb and serve with the tortillas, cilantro, basil, shaved cucumbers, and paprika lime sour cream.

Plan Ahead

Although these tacos do require some advance planning, that also happens to be the beauty of them. All the components can (and should) be prepared ahead of time, which means when lunch or dinner rolls around everything comes together in a snap!

GARLICKY

Coconut Milk–Braised
Pot Roast

3½ pounds boneless, untrimmed chuck roast or boneless short ribs, divided into 4 equal pieces

2 tablespoons canola oil

Kosher salt

Freshly ground black pepper

1 medium onion, diced

6 cloves garlic, minced

2 cups chicken or beef stock

2 tablespoons fresh lime juice

¼ cup finely chopped fresh cilantro, plus more for serving

1 (13.5-ounce) can full-fat coconut milk

½ pound sweet potato, peeled and cut into 1-inch cubes (about 2 cups)

2 large carrots, peeled and cut into 1-inch pieces (about 1½ cups)

4 cups cooked rice, for serving

1 lime, cut into wedges, for serving

SERVES 4

Sex is great and all, but have you ever had a really scrumptious pot roast? The inspiration for this recipe comes from a dish I had in Portugal aptly named "spoon-tender lamb." It was one of the most amazing things I have ever put in my mouth, and I obviously still think about it to this day! In my recipe, I use beef instead of lamb, and although the braising process takes a little bit of time, the anticipation actually makes the final reward of juicy, fall-apart meat all the more glorious. And, as it braises, your house and nose holes will fill with the exhilarating aroma of creamy coconut, garlic, and beefy beef. After the ingredients have had their way with each other in the oven, the once-tough chuck is now luxurious and melt-in-your-mouth tender, while the sweet potatoes and carrots transform into a dreamy, creamy coconut-scented mash. Simply spoon this over some warm rice and I think you'll understand exactly what I mean by my opening question.

| Sear the Beef |

Position a rack in the center of the oven and preheat the oven to 300°F. Thoroughly pat dry each piece of chuck roast with a paper towel. Rub the oil onto the pieces of chuck roast and season all sides with salt and black pepper. Heat a large Dutch oven over medium-high heat. When the Dutch oven is hot, add the chuck roast and cook, undisturbed, until deep golden brown, 3 to 4 minutes on each side. Transfer to a plate.

| Make the Braising Liquid |

In the same Dutch oven over medium-low heat, add the onions and ½ teaspoon each of salt and black pepper. Cook until the onions are translucent and golden brown, 8 to 10 minutes, occasionally scraping the bottom of the pot to loosen any browned bits. Add the garlic and cook until fragrant, 30 to 45 seconds, stirring continuously. Add the stock, lime juice, cilantro, and coconut milk and bring to a boil. Remove from the heat.

| Braise the Ingredients |

Add the sweet potatoes, carrots, and seared chuck roast to the Dutch oven. Give everything a gentle toss in the braising liquid and cover with the lid. Transfer to the oven and braise until the meat is fall-apart tender, 3 to 3½ hours. Skim any fat from the top of the braising liquid and serve hot with cooked rice, lime wedges, and more cilantro.

Sweet Lovin'

Coconut Milk
MOCHI CREPES

1 (13.5-ounce) can full-fat coconut milk

1 cup tapioca flour

¾ cup sweet rice flour (a.k.a. glutinous rice flour)

¼ cup granulated sugar

2 teaspoons pure vanilla extract

½ teaspoon kosher salt

Ice cream, any flavor, for serving (optional)

MAKES 18 SMALL CREPES

Make Ahead

Although these are best eaten immediately, they can be made up to 12 hours ahead of time and kept at room temperature tightly covered in plastic wrap. To serve, warm in the microwave for 15 to 20 seconds (and although they'll lose their crispy edges, they'll still be chewy).

I don't know what it is about chewy treats that makes them so irresistible, but my sisters and I are obsessed. We love gummy bears, yeasted bread, boba, under-baked cookies, mochi, and the list goes on and on. The only thing we like more is food that is both chewy *and* crispy. If you know what I'm talking about or are simply intrigued, my coconut milk mochi crepes are for you! They're made with a combination of tapioca flour and sweet rice flour, so the interior is chewy but the edges are crispy—the perfect balance of both textures. The batter comes together in the same amount of time it takes to fart and is basically foolproof. You can eat the crepes on their own, dip them in chocolate, fill them with peanut butter, or turn them into little ice cream tacos (which is my favorite way of enjoying them). My only suggestion is that you eat them as soon as possible so you can experience that coveted chewy-crispiness.

Make the Batter — Line a baking sheet with parchment paper. In a medium bowl, whisk together the coconut milk, tapioca flour, sweet rice flour, sugar, vanilla, and salt until smooth (the batter will be quite loose).

Cook the Crepes — Heat a large nonstick skillet (or griddle) over medium-high heat. When the skillet is hot, carefully ladle the batter onto the skillet (about 3 tablespoons of batter per crepe). Cook the crepes until tiny bubbles form on the surface and the bottom is golden brown, 1 to 2 minutes. Flip and cook the other side until lightly browned, 1 to 2 minutes. Transfer to the lined baking sheet and continue with the rest of the batter. Serve immediately with ice cream (if using).

Are You All About the Crispy Edges?

Use this batter in a waffle maker! Lightly grease a waffle maker with cooking spray and add ½ cup of batter. Cook until golden brown and crispy, 2 to 4 minutes.

Milk & Honey
PANNA COTTA
with Vanilla Mangoes

PANNA COTTA
2 cups whole milk

1 (.25-ounce) packet unflavored gelatin

1 cup heavy cream

3 tablespoons granulated sugar

3 tablespoons honey

1 tablespoon pure vanilla extract

VANILLA MANGOES
2 mangoes (preferably honey mangoes), peeled and cut into chunks

1 teaspoon pure vanilla extract

SERVES 6

Panna cotta may appear intimidating and snooty on the outside, but it's really just melt-in-your-mouth creamy Jell-O on the inside—only more delicious and decadent. I'm not comparing panna cotta to Jell-O to disrespect it, but to let you know it's hella easy to make. Unlike Jell-O, panna cotta should be soft and custardy, which is why getting the perfect consistency is crucial to this dessert. Luckily for you, I provide the exact liquid-to-gelatin ratio so there's really no way you can mess it up. The panna cotta comes out silky and luscious every time with just a hint of honey sweetness, while the vanilla mangoes add a fun, tropical twist. If for some reason you do mess up this recipe, you can color me impressed because you just achieved the impossible.

Bloom the Gelatin

In a medium saucepan off the heat, add the milk. Evenly sprinkle the gelatin over the milk and let it sit for 5 minutes so the gelatin can soften.

Make the Panna Cotta

Set the saucepan over medium heat and whisk in the heavy cream, sugar, honey, and vanilla. Bring to a simmer while continuously whisking until the gelatin fully dissolves. Remove from the heat and let the mixture cool for 10 to 15 minutes, whisking occasionally. Carefully ladle the panna cotta into six serving glasses and let cool at room temperature for 30 minutes. Cover with plastic wrap and refrigerate until set, at least 8 hours.

Prepare the Mangoes

In a medium bowl, toss together the mangoes and vanilla. Refrigerate until needed. When the panna cotta has set, spoon the vanilla mangoes on top and serve immediately.

Storage

Panna cotta without the mangoes can be covered tightly in plastic wrap and stored in the fridge for up to 7 days.

NO-CHOP
Brown Sugar Cinnamon
PEAR CRISP

½ cup old-fashioned rolled oats

3 tablespoons packed brown sugar (light or dark)

3 tablespoons all-purpose flour

1 teaspoon ground cinnamon

½ teaspoon ground nutmeg

1 teaspoon pure vanilla extract

¼ teaspoon kosher salt

4 tablespoons (½ stick) unsalted butter, melted

3 large ripe pears (preferably Bartlett or d'Anjou since they have thinner skin)

Ice cream, any flavor, for serving

SERVES 6

Pears have always been, and always will be, my first choice when making a fruit crisp. With all due respect to apples and peaches, a perfectly ripened, juicy-licious pear has no rival, especially when it comes to baking. Sadly, I feel that pears are often overlooked because most people just don't let them ripen long enough to reach their full, succulent potential. You're missing out, folks! In this recipe, using ripe pears is the most important step and will ensure that the fruit comes out of the oven perfectly tender with its natural sweetness shining through. The concoction sprinkled on top is the bastard child of a crumble and a chewy oatmeal cookie and pairs perfectly with the tender pear. Plus, putting this dessert together takes less time than making a traditional crisp because there's no chopping involved. The result is a gorgeous dessert guaranteed to impress (and satisfy).

Make the Topping

Position a rack in the center of the oven and preheat the oven to 350°F. In a medium bowl, combine the oats, brown sugar, flour, cinnamon, nutmeg, vanilla, and salt. Drizzle in the melted butter and mix until semicrumbly. Transfer to the fridge to firm up a little until needed.

Bake the Pears

Halve each pear lengthwise and, using a melon baller (or a measuring teaspoon), scoop out the cores. Slice a tiny sliver off the round side of each pear half (to prevent them from wobbling) and arrange them cut side up in a baking dish that's just large enough to fit them all snuggly. Evenly sprinkle the oatmeal topping over the pears and add ¼ cup of water to the bottom of the baking dish. Bake until the topping is deep golden brown and the pears are very tender, 30 to 40 minutes, depending on the size and ripeness of the pears. Serve warm with a scoop of ice cream.

No-Churn Crunchy Dark Chocolate
BLACKBERRY ICE CREAM

2 tablespoons cornstarch

2 cups fresh or frozen blackberries

¼ teaspoon kosher salt

1 (14-ounce) can sweetened condensed milk

1 cup plain Greek yogurt (whole-milk or low-fat)

2 cups heavy cream, very cold

2 teaspoons pure vanilla extract

2 ounces dark chocolate, finely chopped

MAKES 8 CUPS

Anyone who grew up in the Pacific Northwest knows that blackberry bushes are everywhere and all around. And while the Debbie Downers at the Washington State Department of Agriculture call them invasive weeds, I like to call them FREE FRUIT! The biggest and juiciest blackberries were always in the very back near the top of these thorny-ass vines, and since I'm a sucker for big and juicy things, I did whatever it took to get to these beauties—even if it meant my baby-soft skin ended up looking like I just got my ass kicked by an angry kitten. Needless to say, I love blackberries. I also love ice cream. So, I decided to marry the two! Not only is this a flavor you won't find at the store, but the texture is quite different as well. While the yogurt and whipped cream balance out the sweetness of the condensed milk, the tiniest addition of cornstarch results in something that is a cross between ice cream and gelato—silky, smooth, and creamy. Eat it with a spoon, make an ice cream float, or—my personal favorite—scoop it onto an old-school wafery cake cone and lick, lick away!

Make the Base

In a small bowl, make a slurry by whisking together the cornstarch with 2 tablespoons of cold water until smooth. In a small saucepan over medium heat, add the blackberries and salt. Cook until the blackberries completely break down, 4 to 5 minutes, stirring occasionally. Add the cornstarch slurry to the blackberries and stir until thickened slightly. Transfer the warm blackberry mixture to a large bowl and stir in the sweetened condensed milk and yogurt until fully combined. Refrigerate until completely cooled, 20 to 25 minutes.

Make the Ice Cream

In a large bowl, combine the heavy cream and vanilla. Using an electric hand mixer fitted with the whisk attachment, whip on high speed until stiff peaks form, being careful not to overwhip the cream (otherwise it will get lumpy and grainy). Add half of the whipped cream into the chilled blackberry mixture and, using a silicone spatula, gently fold it in until just combined. Fold in the remaining whipped cream along with the dark chocolate until only a few white streaks remain. Scrape the ice cream into an 8 × 8-inch baking dish, cover tightly with plastic wrap, and transfer to the freezer for about 5 hours, or overnight. For the best consistency, transfer the ice cream to the fridge for 20 to 30 minutes to soften before serving.

Matcha Toffee Cookies

6 tablespoons
(¾ stick)
unsalted butter,
softened

½ cup packed light
brown sugar

3 tablespoons honey

2 teaspoons pure
vanilla extract

1 teaspoon matcha
(green tea
powder)

1 cup all-purpose
flour

½ cup milk chocolate
English toffee
bits (such as
crushed Heath
bars) or hard
caramel candy
bits (such
as crushed
Werther's
Original candies)

Flaky sea salt (such
as Maldon), for
sprinkling

MAKES 20 COOKIES

I know what you're thinking: not *another* cookie recipe in a world littered with everyone and their mothers claiming to have the perfect one. I'll straight up admit that these might not be "the best" cookies you've ever had—instead, I humbly offer what might actually be one of the most *interesting* cookies you've ever tasted. These slice-and-bake treats have a satisfying chew thanks to the milk chocolate toffee bits scattered throughout the dough. A pinch of flaky sea salt adds a little savory crunch, while the touch of matcha (green tea powder) provides just enough bitterness to balance everything out. This just might end up being the cookie recipe that you never knew you needed.

Beat the Butter

In the bowl of a stand mixer fitted with the paddle attachment, add the butter, brown sugar, honey, vanilla, and matcha. Beat on high speed until well combined, about 1 minute, scraping down the sides and paddle with a silicone spatula halfway through.

Make the Dough

Add half of the flour to the butter mixture and beat on medium speed until just combined, about 30 seconds. Using the silicone spatula, scrape down the sides and paddle. Add the rest of the flour and beat on medium speed until just combined, about 30 seconds (the dough will look somewhat dry and crumbly, so don't overmix!). Fold in the toffee bits with the spatula until evenly distributed and turn the dough out onto a large piece of plastic wrap. Using your hands, shape the dough into a 10-inch log (doesn't need to be perfect), then wrap tightly in the plastic wrap. Smooth out the dough log by rolling it back and forth a few times on the countertop. Refrigerate until firm, about 2 hours, or overnight. Chilling the dough not only firms it up, but allows the flour to hydrate and fully absorb moisture, so don't skip this step!

Bake the Cookies

Position a rack in the center of the oven and preheat the oven to 350°F. Line a baking sheet with parchment paper (or a Silpat cookie liner). Remove the dough log from the plastic wrap and, using a serrated knife, slice into ½-inch-thick rounds. Arrange the rounds (about 1 inch apart) on the prepared baking sheet. If one of the rounds falls apart, simply press it back together. Sprinkle each round with a pinch of flaky sea salt and gently press the salt into the dough. Bake until the cookies are just set and slightly puffed up, 12 to 13 minutes. Do not be tempted to overbake or they will lose their chewiness!

Storage

Let the cookies cool completely and store in an airtight container at room temperature for up to 3 days (or freeze them for up to 3 months).

SUSHI-RICE PUDDING
with Roasted Grapes

ROASTED GRAPES

½ pound seedless grapes on the vine (red or green), divided into small clusters

2 tablespoons extra-virgin olive oil

½ teaspoon ground cinnamon, plus more for garnish

RICE PUDDING

5 cups whole milk

½ cup uncooked white sushi rice, unrinsed

¼ cup packed brown sugar (light or dark)

½ teaspoon kosher salt

1 tablespoon pure vanilla extract

1 (12-ounce) can evaporated milk

Honey or maple syrup, for drizzling

SERVES 4

When I was a little schoolboy, my mom would buy those giant tubs of rice pudding from Costco and I'd always "accidentally" eat an entire tub that same day. I was a growing boy! Sure, regular pudding is undeniably delicious, but pudding with rice in it is even better since, well, everything's better with rice! In this recipe, I use sushi rice because it's a bit chewier than its cousins, but feel free to use whatever kind of white rice you have in your pantry (whether it's short, medium, or long grain). And to top it off, I garnish the pudding with roasted grapes for an extra pop of sweetness. If you've never had roasted grapes before, they're juicy like fresh grapes, intensely flavored like raisins, and sweet like canned grapes (speaking of, canned grapes are a great substitute). If I had to choose one dessert to eat for the rest of my life, this would be the one.

Roast the Grapes

Position a rack in the center of the oven and preheat the oven to 425°F. Line a rimmed baking sheet with parchment paper. Place the clusters of grapes on the prepared baking sheet and drizzle with the oil. Sprinkle the cinnamon on top and roast until the grapes have puffed up (and a few have burst open), 12 to 14 minutes. Let cool and refrigerate until needed.

Cook the Rice

In a large pot over medium-high heat, combine the milk, sushi rice, brown sugar, and salt. Bring to a gentle boil (keep an eye on this or the milk will bubble over), immediately reduce the heat to a simmer, and cook, uncovered, until the mixture is very thick (almost like mashed potatoes), 45 to 50 minutes, stirring occasionally while scraping the bottom of the pot with a silicon spatula to prevent burning.

Finish the Pudding

Stir in the vanilla and evaporated milk. Bring to a simmer and continue cooking until the pudding resembles the consistency of loose yogurt, 10 to 15 more minutes. Let cool completely and refrigerate until cold (the pudding will thicken even more once cooled). Divide the rice pudding into serving bowls. Garnish with the roasted grapes, a dash of cinnamon, and a drizzle of honey.

Salted UPSIDE-DOWN *Buttermilk* BANANA CAKE

There are people who occasionally eat banana bread, and then there are people who *LOVE* banana EVERYTHING. I definitely fall into the second category because I will gladly stuff a banana anything into my mouth at a moment's notice. This cake is a banana-lover's dream comprised of bananas on top of banana cake filled with banana chunks. The only kind of banana cake I don't like is a dry one, so I use buttermilk in the batter to keep it moist with the ooey-gooey caramelized bananas on top as insurance. To maximize the banana goodness in my cake, I recommend using the ripest, spottiest bananas you can find and making a chunky mash (guaranteeing little pockets of creamy fruit throughout the crumb). Lastly, I strongly suggest serving the cake warm with an oversized scoop of vanilla ice cream. Ummm, yes, please!

**UPSIDE-DOWN
BANANAS**

Cooking spray

6 tablespoons
(¾ stick)
unsalted butter

¼ cup packed brown
sugar (light or
dark)

1 teaspoon pure
vanilla extract

1 teaspoon kosher
salt

2 large very ripe
bananas,
sliced in half
lengthwise and
peeled

CAKE

1½ cups all-purpose
flour

¼ cup granulated
sugar

1 teaspoon baking
soda

½ teaspoon baking
powder

¾ cup buttermilk

3 tablespoons canola
oil

2 large eggs

1 teaspoon pure
vanilla extract

1¼ cups chunky
mashed bananas
(about 3 large
very ripe
bananas)

Vanilla ice cream, for
serving

SERVES 12

| Prep the Bananas | Position a rack in the center of the oven and preheat the oven to 350°F. Grease an 8 × 8-inch baking pan with cooking spray. In a small saucepan over medium heat, add the butter, brown sugar, vanilla, and salt. Cook until the sugar melts and the mixture looks glossy, 2 to 3 minutes (it will begin to bubble, so make sure you monitor this step). Pour the hot butter mixture into the prepared baking pan so that it evenly coats the bottom and arrange the sliced bananas cut side down on top. Set aside. |

| Make the Batter | In a large bowl, whisk together the flour, sugar, baking soda, and baking powder. Whisk in the buttermilk, oil, eggs, and vanilla until just combined. Using a silicone spatula, fold in the mashed bananas until just incorporated (the batter will be pretty thick and chunky). |

| Bake the Cake | Scrape the batter into the prepared pan, spreading it evenly over the halved bananas. Bake until the top is deep golden brown and a toothpick inserted into the center comes out clean, 40 to 45 minutes. Let cool for at least 15 minutes before inverting onto a large serving plate. Slice the cake and serve warm with a scoop (or two) of vanilla ice cream. |

Tip

To get bananas that are perfectly halved lengthwise without breaking them, slice them while they are still in the peel, then carefully remove the peel.

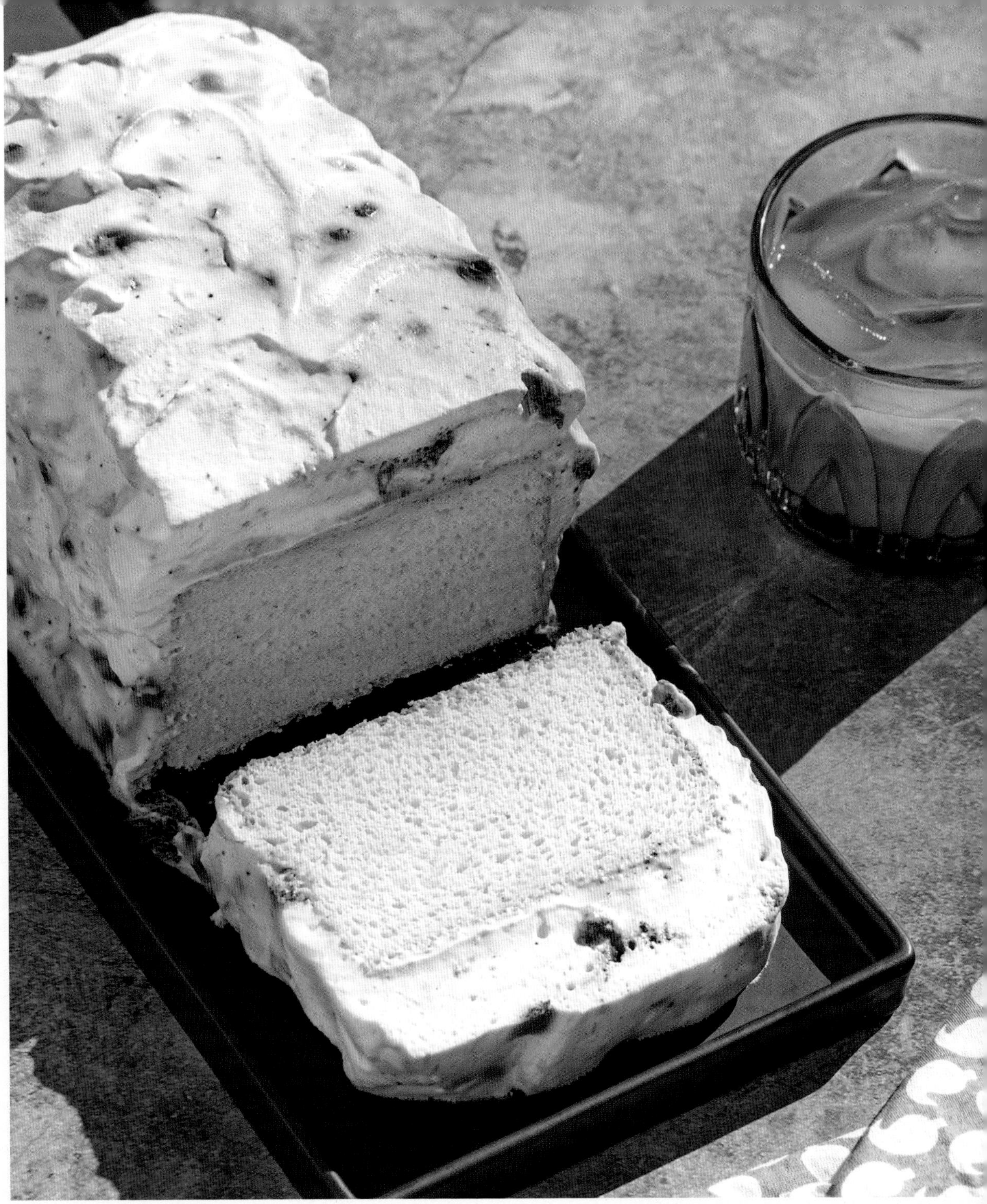

ANGEL FOOD Loaf Cake with Blueberry Whipped Cream

BLUEBERRY WHIPPED CREAM

1 cup fresh or frozen blueberries

2 cups heavy cream, very cold

2 tablespoons granulated sugar

1 teaspoon pure vanilla extract

CAKE

½ cup all-purpose flour

1 tablespoon cornstarch

¾ cup granulated sugar, divided

6 large egg whites, room temperature (no trace of yolk!)

1 tablespoon distilled white vinegar or lemon juice

2 teaspoons pure vanilla extract

½ teaspoon kosher salt

SERVES 8

Do you know what the best thing is about being in a large, close-knit family like mine? And no, it's not the super-fun bickering or hearing my mom list all the reasons why we should be more like our cousins. It's the BIRTHDAY CAKES . . . and in my family there's a constant rotation of Chinese bakery–style cakes. These cakes are usually made with angel food (or sponge) cake layered with airy, not-too-sweet whipped cream and lots of fresh fruit. They're satisfying and delectable yet surprisingly light and delicate. This recipe is a simplified version of one of my favorites, a fluffy angel food cake covered in a lightly sweetened blueberry whipped cream. It's uncomplicated and flawless. Also, there's a rumor going around that I can eat an entire cake in one sitting, and I'm proud to confirm this is 100% true.

Cook the Blueberries
Position a rack in the center of the oven and preheat the oven to 350°F. In a small saucepan over medium heat, add the blueberries and cook until they begin to break down, 3 to 4 minutes. Transfer to a bowl and lightly smash them with a fork. Refrigerate until needed.

Sift the Dry Ingredients
In a medium bowl, sift together the flour, cornstarch, and ¼ cup of the sugar. Set aside. The cornstarch will help make the cake more tender.

Whip the Egg Whites
In a clean, dry bowl of a stand mixer fitted with the whisk attachment, add the egg whites, vinegar, vanilla, and salt. Whip on medium speed until frothy, about 45 seconds. Increase the speed to high and slowly add the remaining ½ cup sugar, 1 tablespoon at a time, until stiff peaks form, 3 to 4 minutes. Alternatively, you can do this with an electric hand mixer (it will just take a little longer).

Add the Dry Ingredients
Using a silicone spatula, gently fold half of the sifted dry ingredients into the whipped egg whites until combined, 14 to 16 folds, making sure to scrape the sides and bottom of the bowl. Fold in the remaining dry ingredients until just combined, another 14 to 16 folds. Scrape the batter into an ungreased 9 x 5-inch loaf pan (it will be very full) and bake until lightly browned and a toothpick inserted into the center comes out clean, 40 to 45 minutes. Cool the cake upside down on a wire rack for 1 hour before unmolding it. In the meantime, make the blueberry whipped cream.

Tip

The quickest way to separate egg yolks from the whites is to use cold eggs and clean, dry hands. Crack the eggs into a bowl and gently lift the egg yolks up with your fingers. Let the whites fall between your fingers back into the bowl. Transfer the yolks to a separate bowl. On the flip side, egg whites whip up better when they're at room temperature. Go figure!

Make the
Blueberry
Whipped
Cream

In a clean, dry bowl of a stand mixer fitted with the whisk attachment, add the heavy cream, sugar, and vanilla. Whip on medium-high speed until stiff peaks form, about 1 minute, being careful not to overwhip; otherwise the cream will become lumpy and grainy. Using a silicone spatula, gently fold the cooled cooked blueberries into the whipped cream until combined, and refrigerate until needed.

Frost the
Cake

To unmold the cake, carefully run a sharp knife along the sides of the cake and gently tap the bottom of the loaf pan until it releases. Transfer the cake to a serving platter and frost with the blueberry whipped cream (be generous!). Using a serrated knife, slice and serve.

Make Ahead

You can assemble the entire cake up to 2 days in advance—just cover it with plastic wrap and store in the fridge. When you're ready to serve, smooth over the whipped topping with a spatula and it will look as good as new!

Creamsicle Cake

with Crunchy Almonds

CAKE

¾ cup granulated sugar

¼ cup unsweetened applesauce

1 large egg

1 tablespoon canola oil

2 teaspoons pure vanilla extract

1 cup all-purpose flour

1 teaspoon baking soda

¼ teaspoon kosher salt

2 cups mandarin orange segments, fresh (peeled and separated) or canned (well drained)

FROSTING

½ cup powdered sugar

4 ounces (½ brick) cream cheese, room temperature

1 tablespoon unsalted butter, softened

1 teaspoon pure vanilla extract

¼ cup sliced or slivered roasted almonds (optional)

SERVES 8

My mom never *ever* made dessert for us growing up. Instead, she'd slice up an orange and call *that* dessert, telling me if I didn't get my vitamin C, I'd catch a cold and die. I really admire Mama Woo's ability to get straight to the takeaway message. Over the years, I've actually come to appreciate the occasional orange for dessert. But I also enjoy *real* desserts because I'm a fully grown adult human who doesn't live with his parents anymore and likes happiness. So, when it comes to orange-themed desserts, this cake is everything you could ever want—complete with juicy orange segments! The crumb is moist and tender and packed full of sweet juicy mandarin oranges, while the thin layer of cream cheese frosting adds just enough of the creaminess you would expect from a cake named after a creamy citrus popsicle. Not a bad way to get your vitamin C if you ask me!

Make the Batter

Position a rack in the center of the oven and preheat the oven to 350°F. Line the inside of a 9 × 5-inch loaf pan with parchment paper. In a large bowl, whisk together the sugar, applesauce, egg, oil, and vanilla until fully combined. Whisk in the flour, baking soda, and salt until just combined. Add the mandarin segments, and, using a silicone spatula, gently fold them into the batter until just combined.

Bake the Cake

Scrape the batter into the prepared loaf pan and bake until the top is deep golden brown and a toothpick inserted into the center comes out clean, 45 to 55 minutes (add 5 to 10 more minutes if you used canned mandarins). Let the cake cool for about 20 minutes while you make the frosting.

Make the Frosting

In a medium bowl, add the powdered sugar, cream cheese, butter, and vanilla. Using an electric hand mixer fitted with the whisk attachment, beat on high speed until smooth and fluffy, about 45 seconds. Unmold the cake from the loaf pan. Evenly spread the frosting on top and sprinkle with the sliced almonds (if using). Slice and serve.

Storage

Leftover cake can be tightly wrapped in plastic wrap and stored in the fridge for up to 3 days.

Fudgy FLOURLESS CHOCOLATE CAKE

with Malted Crème Anglaise & Macerated Strawberries

This is the cake that put The Delicious Cook on the map. And before you make assumptions that this is just another flourless chocolate cake, I need you to know you're wrong. This cake is melt-in-your-mouth tender. Rich and chocolaty. And by far the most popular dessert I've ever made. It is one of my most sacred creations, and I've never ever shared the recipe with anyone . . . until now. The batter has one simple, but essential, secret ingredient (hint: it's heavy cream) that no one else uses, making it the best flourless chocolate cake you will ever put in your mouth! This decadent, fudgy cake is delicious on its own but when served with macerated strawberries and malted crème anglaise, which is French for "fine-ass custard sauce," it transforms into literal dessert perfection.

Make Ahead

The cake, strawberries, and crème anglaise can all be prepared up to 3 days in advance and stored in the fridge. The cake will firm up as it chills, the macerated strawberries will continue to soften with each passing day, and the crème anglaise will thicken in the fridge overnight. You can serve the cake either chilled or at room temperature.

MACERATED STRAWBERRIES

2 cups hulled and halved fresh strawberries

2 tablespoons packed brown sugar (light or dark)

CRÈME ANGLAISE

1 cup heavy cream

2 tablespoons malted milk powder (optional)

2 tablespoons granulated sugar

1 teaspoon pure vanilla extract

1 large egg

1 large egg yolk

FLOURLESS CHOCOLATE CAKE

Cooking spray

1 cup granulated sugar

¼ cup unsweetened cocoa powder, plus more for the pan

1 cup (2 sticks) unsalted butter

½ cup heavy cream

1 cup semisweet chocolate chips

5 large eggs

Powdered sugar, for dusting

SERVES 8

Macerate the Strawberries

In a medium bowl, toss the strawberries and brown sugar until fully combined. Cover with plastic wrap and refrigerate until needed.

Make the Crème Anglaise

In a small saucepan off the heat, whisk together the heavy cream, malted milk powder (if using), sugar, vanilla, egg, and egg yolk until combined. Cook the mixture over medium heat until curdled and thickened, 5 to 7 minutes, whisking often. If it looks like watery scrambled eggs, I promise you that's correct! Let the mixture cool for 5 to 10 minutes, then transfer to a blender and blend until very smooth, about 45 seconds. Pour into a small bowl and let cool. Cover with plastic wrap and refrigerate until needed.

Make the Batter

Position a rack in the center of the oven and preheat the oven to 350°F. Grease an 8-inch springform pan with cooking spray and thoroughly dust the sides and bottom of the pan with cocoa powder. Wrap the bottom half of the outside of the pan with aluminum foil (to prevent leakage). In a medium bowl, whisk together the sugar and cocoa powder until combined. Set aside. In a small saucepan over medium heat, combine the butter and heavy cream and cook until the butter is fully melted, whisking often. Turn the heat off and add the chocolate chips. Whisk until all of the chocolate has melted and the mixture is smooth. Add the chocolate mixture and eggs to the sugar and cocoa mixture. Whisk until smooth.

Bake the Cake

Scrape the batter into the prepared pan and bake until the cake is puffed up and crackly on top (and the center is no longer jiggly), 60 to 65 minutes. As it cools, the center of the cake will collapse, which is completely expected! Let the cake cool completely, then run a sharp thin knife along the side of the pan and unmold. Transfer the cake to a cake stand and dust with powdered sugar. Serve with the macerated strawberries and malted crème anglaise.

Storage

The flourless chocolate cake can be tightly wrapped in plastic wrap and frozen for up to 3 months. And if you want those clean, perfect cake slices, cut the cake while it's still frozen (before letting it come to room temperature).

Pots de Crème

with Salted Graham Cracker Crumble

GRAHAM CRACKER CRUMBLE

1 cup finely crushed graham crackers

¼ cup all-purpose flour

¼ cup packed light brown sugar

3 tablespoons unsalted butter, melted

1 teaspoon ground cinnamon

½ teaspoon kosher salt

POTS DE CRÈME

1 cup milk (low-fat or whole)

¾ cup heavy cream

3 large eggs

2 tablespoons packed brown sugar (light or dark)

¼ teaspoon kosher salt

1 cup semisweet chocolate chips

7 ounces marshmallow crème, for topping

SERVES 6

Chilly night bonfires in big groups were totally a thing when I was in high school. While all the other teenagers thought they were cool drinking cheap beer and playing tonsil hockey with each other, I was busy perfecting my marshmallow game on the open flame. After roasting those sweet pillowy puffs to a perfect golden brown, I'd build a little army of s'mores and walk around shoving them in people's faces—I guess I've just always enjoyed feeding people. S'mores have had a special place in my heart ever since, and those memories are where I draw inspiration for this recipe. These little pots of s'mores heaven are made with a silky, no-bake chocolate "custard" topped with a layer of mega-crunchy graham cracker crumble and a fluffy scoop of toasted marshmallow crème. This dessert screams happiness and teenage dreams in every bite (at least my version of it)!

Make the Crumble

Position a rack in the center of the oven and preheat the oven to 350°F. Line a baking sheet with parchment paper. In a medium bowl, add the crushed graham crackers, flour, brown sugar, butter, cinnamon, salt, and 1 tablespoon of water. Using your hands, mix until fully combined and crumbly. Spread the mixture in an even layer onto the prepared baking sheet and bake until dark golden brown, 10 to 12 minutes. This recipe will make more than you need, so once it's completely cooled, store any remainder in a sandwich bag at room temperature for up to 3 days (it's delicious on Greek yogurt or ice cream).

Make the Pots de Crème

In a medium saucepan off the heat, whisk together the milk, heavy cream, eggs, brown sugar, and salt until combined. Set over medium heat and cook until the mixture thickens and looks kind of curdled, 5 to 6 minutes, whisking often. It will look like wet scrambled eggs and that's correct! Let the mixture cool for 5 to 10 minutes, then transfer to a blender along with the chocolate chips and blend until very smooth, about 1 minute. Carefully divide the mixture into six ramekins (or glasses) and refrigerate, uncovered, until set, about 4 hours, or overnight.

Assemble the Pots de Crème

To assemble, sprinkle a couple tablespoons of the graham cracker crumble on top of each pot de crème followed by a spoonful of the marshmallow crème. These can be assembled up to 2 days in advance, covered with plastic wrap, and stored in the fridge (although the graham cracker crumble may lose some crunchiness). If you have a kitchen torch, lightly toast the top of the marshmallow crème for that bonfire-roasted-marshmallow feel!

Brioche BREAD PUDDING with *Caramel* *Apples* & CHANTILLY CREAM ⇥

This is one of Doug's favorite desserts, which is incredibly ironic because he does things like peel the bread off sandwiches and pick off the "fried part" of fried chicken. Yet when it comes to a dessert made entirely out of bread, he will happily devour an entire serving. The great thing about this recipe is that everything from the chantilly cream (which is really just a fancy term for vanilla whipped cream) to the caramel apples to the custard can be prepped up to a day in advance and stored in the fridge. So when you're ready for the most decadent bread pudding ever, all you have to do is bake and assemble. Which leads me to the delicious fact that this is also a great dish for brunch, because, let's be honest, bread pudding is basically post-dinner French toast.

CHANTILLY CREAM

1 cup heavy cream, very cold

2 tablespoons granulated sugar

1 teaspoon pure vanilla extract

BREAD PUDDING

4 (2-inch-thick) slices brioche (get the softest, fluffiest loaf you can find and slice it yourself)

1 cup whole milk or half-and-half

4 large eggs

2 tablespoons granulated sugar

1 teaspoon pure vanilla extract

½ teaspoon kosher salt

CARAMEL APPLES

2 medium apples, peeled, cored, and diced (about 2 cups)

2 tablespoons unsalted butter

2 tablespoons packed brown sugar (light or dark)

Powdered sugar, for dusting

SERVES 4

Make the Chantilly Cream

Position a rack in the center of the oven and preheat the oven to 350°F. In a medium bowl, combine the heavy cream, sugar, and vanilla. Using an electric hand mixer fitted with the whisk attachment, whip on medium-high speed until soft peaks form, 2 to 3 minutes. Cover with plastic wrap and refrigerate until needed.

Toast the Brioche

Arrange the brioche slices in a 9 × 13-inch baking dish, making sure to leave about 1 inch between each slice, and bake until light golden brown, 8 to 10 minutes. This step will help the bread pudding hold its shape later on. Let cool completely. Leave the oven on while you make the custard.

Make the Custard

In a medium bowl, whisk together the milk, eggs, sugar, vanilla, and salt until the sugar dissolves. Once the toasted brioche has cooled, pour all the custard mixture directly onto the baked brioche slices and into the baking dish. Let the brioche soak at room temperature until the custard has been absorbed by the brioche, about 20 minutes, flipping each piece halfway through. While the brioche is soaking, make the caramel apples.

Make the Caramel Apples

In a saucepan over medium heat, combine the apples, butter, and brown sugar. Cook until the apples are just tender and the mixture has thickened slightly, 8 to 10 minutes, stirring occasionally. Remove from the heat and set aside until needed.

Bake the Pudding

Once all the custard has been absorbed, transfer the entire baking dish to the oven and bake until the brioche is puffed up and the edges are golden brown, 20 to 25 minutes. Before serving, dust with powdered sugar and top with the caramel apples. Serve warm with a dollop of the chantilly cream.

Tip

If you're using the end pieces of a brioche loaf, make sure you slice off a thin layer of crust so the crumb is exposed; otherwise the bread might not soak up the custard.

Caramelized Hong Kong–Inspired EGG TART

Cooking spray

1 (10 x 10-inch) sheet
frozen puff
pastry, thawed
in the fridge
overnight

¾ cup evaporated
milk

¾ cup cold water

½ cup packed light
brown sugar

1 teaspoon pure
vanilla extract

⅛ teaspoon kosher
salt

3 large eggs

1 large egg yolk

2 tablespoons salted
butter, melted

Powdered sugar, for
dusting

SERVES 8

One of my favorite ways to end an afternoon of dim sum is with an order of Hong Kong–style egg tarts, also known as "dan tat" in Cantonese. These delectable little treats are usually found in the form of small-to-medium tartlets at dim sum restaurants or Chinese bakeries, but unless you're a professional baker, making them can be a pain in the booty cheeks. That's why my totally bastardized version calls for making a single large tart, resulting in a much easier, one-and-done baking experience. While classic dan tat is a bright, glossy yellow, my version emerges from the oven a beautiful, caramelized golden brown, which is a direct result of blending the batter with brown sugar until it's light and frothy. My recipe might cut some corners compared to the traditional version, but it sacrifices nothing in terms of texture or flavor. The custard is rich and silky smooth with subtle hints of caramel, while the shortcut puff pastry crust is enhanced with a brush of melted salted butter, making it akin to homemade pastry. While it may look different than the traditional dan tat, this version, as I'm reminded after one bite, is actually better . . . and because it's so easy to make, I can enjoy it whenever I want.

| Prepare the Crust | Position a rack in the center of the oven and preheat the oven to 375°F. Grease a 9-inch fluted tart pan (preferably with a removable bottom) with cooking spray. Lay the puff pastry on a large piece of parchment paper and, using a rolling pin, flatten until large enough to cut out an 11-inch round. Using a sharp knife, cut the puff pastry into an 11-inch round and carefully invert it into the tart pan. Peel off the parchment paper and gently press the puff pastry into the pan, making sure to leave a ½-inch overhang on the edges (as the dough will slightly shrink during baking). Transfer to the fridge to chill for at least 10 minutes, or until needed. |

Make the Filling	In a blender, add the evaporated milk, cold water, brown sugar, vanilla, salt, eggs, and egg yolk. Blend until frothy and the sugar has dissolved, 30 to 45 seconds. Place the chilled puff pastry–lined tart pan on a large rimmed baking sheet (this will make it easier to transfer to the oven) and carefully pour the filling (including the froth) into the tart pan about three-quarters of the way up.
Bake the Tart	Carefully transfer the tart pan to the oven and bake until dark golden brown on top and the filling is set, 35 to 40 minutes (it will still jiggle ever so slightly). Brush the crust with melted salted butter and cool for 10 to 15 minutes before slicing. Dust with powdered sugar and serve warm.
Storage	Cover any remaining egg tart with plastic wrap and refrigerate for up to 3 days (it's just as delicious when cold!).

Acknowledgments

Thank you to my two powerhouse literary agents, Steve Troha and Jeff Kleinman, for believing in me and my potential as an author. You helped me hone my voice and find the perfect home for my first book. You are unbelievably amazing and I am forever grateful to you. Thank you, Kat Odom-Tomchin, for all your support and keeping everything so well organized and manageable.

A huge, HUGE thank-you to my editor, Sarah Kwak, who championed my book from the very beginning. I could not have asked for a better partner throughout this entire process. You've always understood my personality and vision for this book! Thank you to the rest of the diverse group of kick-ass boss people at HarperCollins: Tai Blanche, Shelby Peak, Heather Rodino, Aryana Hendrawan, Francesca Carlos, and Anwesha Basu. Thank you for believing in me and my book and helping me make this lifelong dream a reality. Thank you to Laura Palese, my book designer. You are so incredibly talented and creative, and I'm honored that you agreed to design my first book. I love it so much!!!

To Teresa Cendreda, Michelle Pulfrey, Jamie Krell, Steve Rosso, Danielle Kartes, and Sandra Westerman, I will never forget your generosity and willingness to go out on a limb for me. Thank you to my amazing friends who were sweet enough to be my recipe testers, taste testers, and hand models: Cathleen Richland, Jenn Tan, Casey Kopp, Leslie Romero, Jackie Chu, Kellyn Muller, Alexis Longinotti, Amy Blescia-Cascarina, Kevin Mercer, Theresa Morelli, Lindsey Luke, Allison Foster, and Terry Foster. This book would not have been possible without you!

Thank you to Anita Surendran for always supporting me and having my back. You are one of my best friends, who also happens to be the best attorney in the world. To Justin Hecht for keeping me sane!! To Chad Strahan, good things seem to happen whenever you are involved with something (and thank you for making me presentable for the photos in this book)! Thank you, Lisa Hennings, for being the dog whisperer that you are and for putting up with all my crazy requests! I'm so grateful to have all of you in my life!!

To Danielle Kim, Andrew Chason, and Jacob Weisman, thank you for always hustling on my behalf and helping me achieve my dreams. I truly appreciate you!

Thank you to my amazing in-laws (Mama Mac, Papa Mac, Tracey, JG, JMac, Andrea, Jack, Devan, Lauren, and Patrick) for welcoming me and accepting me into the family from the moment we met. It means the world to me, and I could not have asked for a better second family.

Thank you, Dad, for always supporting me no matter what I wanted to do with my life and making sure I always had my eye on the prize. Thank you for taking every single one of my crazy dreams seriously and always doing everything in your power to give me the best possible chance to succeed in life. To Mom, for showing me love through your food and unintentionally teaching me how to give zero f*cks. Thanks for always keeping me well fed and for being the inspiration behind the title of this book. Thank you to my sisters, Melis and Kare, for always being on my team, keeping me grounded, and accepting me no matter what. Thanks, Jake, for being an awesome brother-in-law and possibly loving food even more than I do. Thank you to Addie, Charlotte, and Levi for being the most amazing kids that ever existed and for always wanting to try a thousand different recipes with me every time we hang out. It means everything to me that I'm your favorite uncle in the whole wide world.

To Team Cuddles (a.k.a. Taco, Queso, and Unagi), for your unconditional love, making me laugh throughout the day and letting me smother you with endless kisses. And for the record, I'm totally okay with the fact that you love your other daddy more than me (because I do too). And thank you to Frida, the original love of my life, who opened my heart to even more love. I think about you every day. Dogs are truly the best.

Finally, thank you to my husband, Douglas. You are the love of my life and my best friend in the entire universe. None of this would have been possible without you because you make me feel like I can truly accomplish anything. You are the most amazing human being in the entire galaxy, and I'm lucky that you are all mine. Thank you for being my biggest fan, biggest believer, biggest supporter, biggest cheerleader, biggest heart . . . basically, you're my biggest everything. You bring out the best in me (and happen to know all my best angles too)! I must have been a world-saving saint in another lifetime because I have no idea how I landed you in this one. I love you more than you will ever know (just remember this if you ever think about leaving me!). And one more thing—we made a cookbook!!

Index

NOTE: Page references in *italics* indicate photographs.